DO ANDROIDS DREAM
OF ELECTRIC SHEEP?

Rick Deckard is an android killer. He works for the police in San Francisco, where the deadly radioactive dust from World War Terminus still covers the city like a grey cloud, blocking out the sun. Nearly all the animals in the world have died, and most people have emigrated to Mars, where the government gives them androids to work as servants. But some androids escape and return, illegally, to Earth.

There are six escaped androids on Rick's list. He must search for them through the dusty, half-deserted city, use tests to identify them as non-human, then shoot them down with his laser gun. He earns a thousand dollars for each killing. Perhaps, he thinks, he'll soon be able to buy a real living animal with his earnings, instead of the electric sheep he owns now.

But these are Nexus-6 androids. They breathe, move, look, sound like humans; they have ten million electrical connections in their brains and think faster than many people. They're intelligent, dangerous, and hard to kill.

Rick Deckard will earn every cent of his six thousand dollars. If he lives.

D1378052

OXFORD BOOKWORMS LIBRARY

Fantasy & Horror

Do Androids Dream of Electric Sheep?

Stage 5 (1800 headwords)

Series Editor: Jennifer Bassett
Founder Editor: Tricia Hedge
Activities Editors: Jennifer Bassett and Christine Lindop

PHILIP K. DICK

Do Androids Dream of Electric Sheep?

Retold by
Andy Hopkins and Joc Potter

OXFORD UNIVERSITY PRESS

OXFORD
UNIVERSITY PRESS

Great Clarendon Street, Oxford OX2 6DP

Oxford University Press is a department of the University of Oxford.
It furthers the University's objective of excellence in research, scholarship,
and education by publishing worldwide in

Oxford New York

Auckland Cape Town Dar es Salaam Hong Kong Karachi
Kuala Lumpur Madrid Melbourne Mexico City Nairobi
New Delhi Shanghai Taipei Toronto

With offices in

Argentina Austria Brazil Chile Czech Republic France Greece
Guatemala Hungary Italy Japan Poland Portugal Singapore
South Korea Switzerland Thailand Turkey Ukraine Vietnam

OXFORD and OXFORD ENGLISH are registered trade marks of
Oxford University Press in the UK and in certain other countries

ISBN 978 0 19 479222 6

Printed in Hong Kong

ACKNOWLEDGEMENTS
Illustrated by: Stephen Player

Word count (main text): 31,300 words

For more information on the Oxford Bookworms Library,
visit www.oup.com/elt/bookworms

CONTENTS

1

The challenge

Rick Deckard woke up to the sound of the alarm from the mood machine beside his bed. He got up and stretched. In her own bed, his wife Iran opened her sad, grey eyes, frowned, and then shut them again.

'Your mood machine is on too weak,' he said to her. 'If I turn it up for you, you'll be awake and . . .'

'Don't touch my mood settings.' Her voice was sharp and bitter. 'I don't *want* to be awake.'

He sat down on her bed, bent over her and explained softly, 'At a high enough setting, you'll be *glad* you're awake; that's the whole point.' He touched her shoulder gently – *his* setting had been high and he was in a good mood.

'Get that policeman's hand away from me,' Iran said.

'I'm not a policeman.' He felt cross, although he hadn't dialled the mood machine for crossness.

'You're worse than a policeman,' his wife said, her eyes still shut. 'You're a murderer working for the police.'

'I've never killed a human being in my life.' He was really angry now.

'Only those poor androids.'

'You've always been happy to spend the money I earn.' He stood up and walked across the room to his mood machine.

1

'Instead of saving,' he added, 'so we can buy a real sheep in place of that fake electric one upstairs.' He wondered whether to dial for a happier mood or for an angrier one that would allow him to win the argument.

'If you dial for more anger,' Iran said, eyes open and watching, 'then I'll dial the same. We'll have the biggest fight that we've ever had. Just try me.' She got up quickly and moved towards her own mood machine.

Rick gave in. 'What's on your timetable for today?' he asked, dialling his own to check it.

'It lists a six-hour depression,' Iran said.

'What? Why did you timetable that?' It defeated the whole purpose of the mood machine. 'I didn't even know there *was* a setting for depression,' he said miserably.

'I was watching Buster Friendly on television one afternoon,' Iran said. 'During the advertisements I turned off the sound for a minute, and I heard this building . . .'

'The empty apartments.' Rick understood immediately. Sometimes he heard them at night. But their building was actually half-full. Others, in areas that before the war were called the suburbs, were now completely empty. He had heard this, anyway; he did not want to experience it directly.

'I was in a 382 mood at the time,' Iran went on, 'so I heard the emptiness but I didn't feel it. At first I was grateful that I had a mood machine. But then I realized that it was unhealthy *not* to react to the absence of life. So I found a setting for depression and I put it on my timetable for twice a month. I can spend that time thinking about life here on Earth, now that anybody with any intelligence has emigrated. That's reasonable, don't you think?'

'But in that kind of mood it's difficult to dial something different. You'll just stay depressed.'

'I put a 481 on the timetable for six hours later,' Iran explained. 'New hope, awareness of . . .'

'I know 481,' he said. He had dialled it many times. He took his wife's hands. 'Listen. Cancel the depression. It's dangerous. I must go soon, but come into the other room now and watch some television with me.'

'I hate watching television before breakfast.'

'Dial 888,' Rick said, as he went into the living-room and turned the television on. 'Then you'll want to watch it.'

He turned up the sound and the voice of Buster Friendly filled the room. Iran came in and turned it off again.

'OK, I'll dial,' she said. 'Any mood you want. What difference does it make?'

'I'll dial for both of us,' Rick said. In the bedroom he dialled 594 for her (happy awareness of her husband's greater common sense) and for himself a fresh and businesslike interest in his job.

After a quick breakfast, Rick put on his protective clothing and hurried up to the roof garden. His electric sheep was chewing calmly, just like a normal sheep in a field of grass. The neighbours, of course, never asked if it was a fake. The question 'Is your sheep real?' would be even ruder than 'Are those your own teeth?'.

The morning sky was grey with radioactive dust and he could smell death in the air. But it was not so bad now. People like him who had lived through World War Terminus were the strong ones. The dust continued to have its effects on their minds and their bodies, but police hospital tests showed that Rick was a 'regular' – he could still have children. If you failed the test, you became a 'special', and every day new specials were created from regulars by the dust. 'Emigrate now!' the government advertisements ordered. But I can't emigrate, Rick said to himself, because of my job.

Bill Barbour, the owner of the next garden, greeted him. Barbour was checking his horse. 'I'll have two soon,' he said, pointing to the horse's stomach.

He found the hidden door of the control box, and opened it.

4

'Can I buy the baby from you?' Rick asked quickly. He hated owning a fake animal but followers of Mercerism, the official religion, had to have one if they couldn't afford a real animal.

'Sorry. They're Percherons. I want to keep them both.'

Rick reached into his pocket and took out his bent copy of Sidney's, the official guide to all animal prices. He found the page for horses.

'I can buy a young Percheron horse from Sydney's for five thousand dollars,' he said aloud.

'No, you can't,' Barbour said. 'Look again. That would be the price if they had any, but they haven't.'

'I could pay you five hundred dollars a month for ten months,' Rick suggested.

'Sorry, Deckard,' Barbour replied. 'Before the war there were hundreds of these Percherons, but now . . . I had to fly to Canada for this one and drive her back myself so that she wasn't stolen. Then I had to pay a fortune for the frozen eggs, to produce the baby.'

'But if you have two horses and I haven't got one, that's against the whole idea of Mercerism.'

'You have your sheep. There are about fifty families in this building – one for every three apartments – and every family has an animal. Even Ed Smith has a cat, although nobody's ever seen it.'

Rick bent down and searched in the thick, white wool of his sheep. He found the hidden door of the control box, and opened it.

'Look,' he said to Barbour. 'Do you understand now why I want that horse so badly? I care about this sheep, but it's not the same. I'm always afraid that someone in the building will notice when it breaks down. The repair man is very careful and dresses in white like an animal doctor, but . . . You know what people are like if you're not looking after a real animal. It's not a crime now, but I still feel like a criminal.'

Barbour stared at the controls and then looked at Rick sympathetically. 'I'm really sorry,' he said. 'Why don't you buy a cat? They're cheap.'

'I want a large animal,' Rick answered. 'I had a real sheep once, but it died.' If he killed five androids, he thought, he would get a thousand dollars for each on top of his normal salary. But there were too many android killers around. 'I have to get to work,' he told his neighbour. His mind was now on his job, on the day ahead.

On his way to work, Rick, like so many other people, stopped outside one of San Francisco's larger pet shops. In the centre of the long shop window stood an ostrich in a heated plastic cage. It was, Rick knew, the only ostrich on the West Coast. He spent a few minutes staring at the price, and as a result he was late arriving for work at the police station.

While he was unlocking his office door, his boss, Police Inspector Harry Bryant, appeared at his side.

'I want to see you at nine thirty in Dave Holden's office,' Inspector Bryant told him. 'Holden,' he added, 'is in Mount Zion Hospital. Half his backbone was blown away by a laser gun. It'll be a month, at least, before they can fit him with a new plastic one.'

'What happened?' Rick asked, shocked. Holden had been fine the day before.

'Nine thirty,' Bryant repeated, and walked away.

Rick entered his own office. Holden was one of the best. His attacker must have been one of the new super-intelligent androids with the Nexus-6 brain. Most police forces were protesting about them, in Russia as well as across America. The company that had developed the Nexus-6 was difficult to control, though, because its main factory was on the planet Mars.

Rick took a large brown envelope from his desk drawer, then looked at the time. It was still only nine fifteen and the ostrich in the shop window was still fresh in his mind. He picked up the phone.

'Happy Dog Pet Shop,' a voice answered and a tiny happy face slowly appeared on the video screen. Rick could hear the sounds of animals in the background.

'The ostrich in your window,' Rick said, playing with a pen on his desk. 'How much would the first payment be?'

'Let's see . . .' the animal salesman said. 'One third of the full price. Then you pay the rest over thirty months at . . .'

'Take two thousand off the price, and I'll pay cash,' Rick said. With Dave Holden out of action, he could earn a lot in the next month.

'Sir, the price is already low,' the salesman told him. 'Check your Sydney's.'

Rick pulled it out of his pocket again and found the page for ostriches.

'Male, excellent condition,' the salesman continued. 'Thirty thousand dollars. Now, about that first payment . . .'

'I'll think about it,' Rick said, 'and call you back.' He started to hang up.

'Your name, sir?' the salesman asked quickly.

'Frank Merriwell,' Rick told him, and invented an address.

All that money, he thought, as he hung up. But some people have enough to buy them. He dialled the number of the false-animal shop where he had bought his sheep.

'Dr McRae.' The figure of the man himself appeared more slowly.

'This is Deckard. How much is an electric ostrich?'

'Oh, I think we could make you one for under eight hundred dollars. How soon do you want it? We . . .'

'I'll talk to you later,' said Rick. 'Goodbye.'

He put the phone down, feeling depressed. His eyes fell on the brown envelope in front of him and he looked through it until he found what he wanted: all the most recent information on the Nexus-6.

The figures were extraordinary. The Nexus-6 had a choice of ten million separate electrical pathways in its brain; in less than a second these androids could react in one of at least fourteen different ways. They were more intelligent than some classes of human specials, so no intelligence test would trap them. The only hope of recognizing them was by using the Voigt-Kampff Empathy Test; only humans were capable of feeling empathy with other life forms. Rick, and other followers of Mercerism, had no problem experiencing the feelings of other living creatures. Humanlike androids did not have this quality. They stood alone, so they were considered killers. Rick and his colleagues could kill them without breaking the laws of Mercerism.

It was already nine thirty. Rick quickly put the papers back in the envelope and hurried to Holden's room. Inspector Bryant was already in there, using the videophone.

'I see you've brought the information on the Nexus-6,' Bryant said, putting the phone down as Rick entered.

'Yes, I thought it must be them,' Rick answered. 'How many androids are involved and how far did Dave get?'

'There were eight to start with,' Bryant said, checking Holden's notes, which were on the desk in front of him. 'Dave killed the first two.'

'And the others are here in Northern California?'

'Dave thinks so. That was him on the phone.'

'I'm ready to take Dave's place,' Rick offered.

Bryant thought for a moment.

'Dave used the Voigt-Kampff Test on those he suspected. You realize that the test was not prepared specially for the Nexus-6? No test has been.' He paused. 'Dave thinks it's accurate. Maybe it is. But before you look for the other six, I want you to fly to the Rosen Corporation in Seattle and talk with the people who made them.'

'And test the new androids?'

'Yes. I'm going to phone the company now and discuss the possibility of including several humans in the tests. You won't know which ones they are.' Bryant suddenly pointed his finger at Rick. His face was serious. 'This is a very responsible job. Dave has a lot of experience behind him.'

'So have I,' Rick said.

'Your jobs usually come through Dave. He chooses them carefully. But now you've got six that he intended to kill himself, and one of them shot him first. Max Polokov. That's what it calls itself. If Dave was right, of course – his list of names is only as accurate as the Voigt-Kampff Test itself. And so far the test has only been given to the first three, the two Dave killed and then Polokov. Dave was giving the test when Polokov lasered him.'

'Then Dave was right,' said Rick.

'Go to Seattle,' Bryant ordered. 'Take a station car.'

Rick stood up.

'Can I take Dave's notes with me?' he asked. 'I want to read them on the way.'

'Let's wait until you've tried that test,' Bryant said.

His voice was not encouraging, Rick noted uneasily. He stood up, feeling miserable. But Dave's sudden disappearance from work meant he could earn six thousand dollars if he killed all six androids. He should be pleased. He breathed deeply for a moment and then turned his mind to Seattle.

2

Seattle

When Rick landed the police hovercar on the roof of the Rosen Corporation Building, a young woman was waiting for him there. She was a thin woman with black hair and she was wearing thick glasses to protect herself from the dust. She did not look happy to see him.

'I'm Rachael Rosen,' she said, holding out her hand. 'I guess you're Mr Deckard.'

'This wasn't my idea,' he answered.

'Yes, Inspector Bryant told us that. But you're here for the San Francisco police, and the police never believe that we're working to help the public.'

'Androids can be useful one moment and dangerous the next. They're not a problem for us as long as they serve their true purpose,' Rick said.

'But when they're considered dangerous, it's your job to kill them, isn't it, Mr Deckard?' said Rachael Rosen coldly.

'Have you chosen the group for me?' Rick asked. He had no wish to discuss his job with the woman. 'I'd like to . . .'

He stopped as he noticed the animals behind her. He had never seen so many in one place. The cages were guarded by men in company uniforms with machine guns, and the men's eyes were watching Rick carefully. He checked his Sydney's

11

guide. Some of those animals did not even have a price. The owl, for example. He stared at the bird, then realized that the girl was speaking again.

'We don't buy from Sydney's or any animal dealer,' she was saying. 'We buy from private individuals. That's why the prices we pay aren't listed.'

Rick just stood there in silence. He remembered the time, in his childhood, when animal after animal started disappearing from the Earth for ever. He thought too about his own need for a real animal. An electric sheep was nothing – nothing at all. It had no feelings and did not even know that he existed. For the first time Rick realized that in many ways electric animals were actually very similar to androids.

'What kind of animal do *you* have?' Rachael's voice seemed a long way away.

'A sheep,' he answered slowly.

'Well, then you should be happy.'

'I *am* happy,' he said. 'But I'd love to own an owl.' He pointed at the bird in front of him. 'I always wanted one, even before they all died . . . All except yours, that is.' He turned away. 'I'd like to do the tests now. Can we go downstairs?'

'I expect Uncle Eldon has arranged everything by now,' Rachael replied without expression. She turned her back and walked towards the door. Rick followed her, surprised that the large corporation was in fact a family business.

'Why don't you like me?' he asked Rachael while they travelled down together to the lower floors.

'If your test doesn't work, we'll have to take all Nexus-6 types off the market.' Her black eyes were fierce now as she frowned at him. 'Just because you police aren't able to do the simple job of recognizing the tiny number that get out of control.'

An older man was waiting for them downstairs. He had a worried expression on his face.

'I'm Eldon Rosen,' he explained to Rick. They shook hands. 'This is very short notice, but we've done the best we can.'

Rick became more confident. They're afraid of me, he realized. I *can* probably stop them producing the Nexus-6, and that could have a serious effect on the future of the corporation.

The Rosens led him into a small room full of beautiful furniture. He sat down next to an expensive-looking coffee table and took out his Voigt-Kampff instruments. 'You can send in the first testee,' he informed Eldon Rosen, who was looking more and more anxious.

'What do those instruments measure?' Rachael asked.

'They measure tiny movements in the eye muscles and under the skin of the face when people are shocked by something that's said to them. It doesn't matter what people actually *say* – it's the physical reactions that they can't control which are important.'

'Give me the test,' Rachael ordered.

'Why?' Rick asked, puzzled.

'We chose her as a testee,' Eldon Rosen answered. 'She may be an android. We're hoping you can tell.' He lit a cigarette and sat down to watch.

Rick attached wires to Rachael's face and shone a thin white light into her left eye. Then he sat in front of his instruments.

'I'm going to talk about a number of situations,' he told

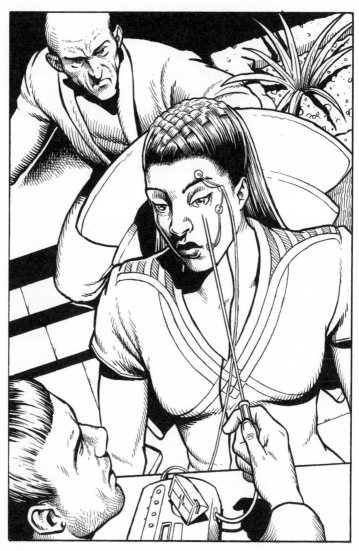

An android reaction, he said to himself.

Rachael. She seemed calm. 'I want you to tell me how you feel about each one as quickly as possible.' Rick chose question three. 'Right. You are given a leather wallet on your birthday.'

The needles on his instruments immediately moved up past the green and into the red, then down again.

'I wouldn't accept it,' Rachael said. 'And I'd report the person who gave it to me to the police.'

Rick made notes and then continued. 'You have a little boy and he shows you his insect collection, including his killing bottle.'

'I'd take him to the doctor.' Rachael's voice was low but confident. The needles moved again, but not so far. He made another note.

'In a magazine you see a full-page colour picture of a girl, wearing no clothes.' Rick paused.

'Are you testing whether I'm an android or whether I like women?' Rachael asked sharply. The needles did not move.

He continued: 'Your husband likes the picture.' Still no reaction. 'The girl,' he added, 'is lying on a large and beautiful sheepskin carpet.' Nothing. An android reaction, he said to himself. Her mind is not on the dead animal. 'Your husband hangs the picture on the wall of his study,' he finished, and this time the needles moved.

'I wouldn't let him,' Rachael said.

'OK,' Rick answered. 'Now, you're reading a book written in the old days before the war. The characters become hungry and go to a seafood restaurant. One of them orders lobster and they all watch while the cook drops the lobster, alive, into boiling water.'

'Oh!' Rachael said. 'That's awful! Did they really do that?'

15

A correct spoken reaction, but the needles did not move. Rick asked a few more questions to check that he was right.

'You're an android,' he told her – or it. He turned to Eldon Rosen, who was looking angry as well as anxious. 'I'm right, aren't I?' he asked. There was no answer. 'Look,' he said, 'we both want this test to work.'

'She's not an android,' Rosen said.

'I don't believe it.'

'Why would he lie?' Rachael said to Rick fiercely.

'I can explain why my niece failed your empathy test,' the old man said. 'She was born on a spaceship and lived there for fourteen of her eighteen years. All she knew about Earth came from the nine other people on the ship, and from cassettes.'

'Outside this building, you would kill me,' Rachael said to Rick. 'I've known that since I arrived on Earth.'

'What were your orders,' Eldon Rosen asked, 'if your test results showed a human as an android?'

'To stop the testing,' Rick replied, packing his instruments away again. 'The test has failed.' Bryant was right, he thought. *I could have killed an innocent person using this test.* 'The problem,' he went on, 'is that you continue to make androids that are more and more like humans, so now . . .'

'We only make what people who emigrate want,' Eldon Rosen said. 'If *we* don't make them, other companies will. Your Voigt-Kampff test was a failure before we produced the Nexus-6 android. You've probably killed other people with underdeveloped empathy reactions, like my niece here. The police are the ones with the problem, not us.'

'So now I'll never be able to test a Nexus-6,' Rick realized. 'The test is useless.'

16

'That's right, Mr Deckard,' Rachael Rosen agreed. Then she smiled. 'And if you can't use the test, you can't find the androids, or kill them, or earn your money.'

'Your boss, Inspector Bryant,' Eldon Rosen said, 'won't understand why you let us defeat your test before it began. But don't worry, Mr Deckard. I'm sure that together we can find a way for you to continue to do your work.'

'Would you really like to own an owl?' Rachael asked Rick.

'I don't think I'll ever have one,' Rick replied, but he knew what she meant. He was starting to realize the kind of business that the Rosen Corporation wanted to do with him.

'You *almost* own an owl,' Rachael continued. 'You can have it. But if it ever has any babies, they'll be ours. Take half an hour to think about it.' She and Eldon Rosen moved towards the door.

'You've trapped me,' Rick said angrily. They stopped and looked back at him. 'You know that my job depends on being able to use the Voigt-Kampff test, and you know that I want your owl.'

'*Your* owl, dear,' replied Rachael. 'It's all yours. Have you decided then?'

It, Rick thought. She's calling the owl it, not her. 'I want,' he said, 'to ask you one more question. Sit down again.'

Rachael looked at her uncle and then returned to her seat. Rick put his black leather bag on the table, took out his instruments, and attached the wires to Rachael's face.

'Do you like my bag?' he asked her, as he searched for his question papers inside it.

'Yes, yes,' she answered, without interest.

'It's made from the skin of human babies,' Rick explained.

There was a pause, and then the needles moved violently. Too late. There should have been no reaction time. 'Thanks, Miss Rosen,' he said, and put everything away again. 'That's all.'

'You're leaving?' Rachael asked.

'Yes,' he said. 'You're an android, and the test works. Does she know?' he asked Eldon Rosen, who was looking very unhappy. Sometimes androids didn't know, because false memories were programmed into their brains.

'No. But I think towards the end, when you asked for another try, she had a good idea. Didn't you?' he asked the girl.

'Yes,' Rachael answered. Her voice was expressionless.

'Don't be afraid of him,' Eldon Rosen told her. 'You belong to the Rosen Corporation and the police can't touch you.'

'He's right,' Rick said. 'I'm not going to kill you, Miss Rosen. Good day.' He started towards the door and then paused. To the two of them he said, 'Is the owl real?'

'No, it's false,' Eldon Rosen answered. 'There are no owls.'

Rick left the room and closed the door behind him. So that's how these people succeed in business, he said to himself. But Rachael must be a Nexus-6. I've seen one for the first time. The test nearly failed – and it's the only way that we have to trap them. The Rosen Corporation certainly tries hard to protect its androids. And I have to find six more of them.

He would earn his money. Every cent. If he lived.

3

Neighbours

In a great empty apartment building far from the centre of San Francisco a single television played. Before World War Terminus the building had been well looked after, but now the owner of these and other apartments had died or emigrated to other planets. There were few people left to miss them.

Nobody really remembered why the war had started or who, if anyone, had won. The radioactive dust that covered the Earth had come from no country and nobody had planned it. After the war the animals had died, the sun had stopped shining, and most people were encouraged to emigrate. Under United Nations law each person who left was given an android to work for them. It became easy to go and very difficult to stay. The few thousands who remained moved into areas where they could live together and see each other. There were only a few odd individuals who stayed alone in the suburbs. John Isidore, listening to the television as he shaved, was one of these.

'Let's hear from Mrs Maggie Klugman,' the television presenter was saying. 'She emigrated to Mars a short time ago. Mrs Klugman, how does your exciting life in New New York compare with the difficulties of your previous life on Earth?'

There was a pause, and then a tired middle-aged voice said, 'Oh, it's wonderful to have an android that you can depend on. And before we left, my husband and I were always worried that we might become specials. Now our worries have gone for ever.'

For me too, John Isidore thought, and I didn't have to emigrate. He had been a special now for over a year. Since he had failed even a basic intelligence test, the popular name for him and others like him was 'chickenhead'. But he survived. He had a job driving a truck for a false-animal repair company, and Mr Sloat, his boss, accepted him as a human being. There were chickenheads who were much more stupid than Isidore.

'So your husband was never confident,' continued the presenter, 'that his protective clothing would . . .'

Isidore had finished shaving, and turned the television off. Silence. It came from the walls, the floor, the ceiling, and from all the machines in the apartment that had stopped working years before. He experienced the silence with his eyes as well as his ears. It almost felt alive.

Did other people feel this emptiness, or only specials like himself? He wanted to ask someone, but there was nobody to ask. There were a thousand apartments in the building, all uninhabited and slowly falling down. In the end they would be buried under the dust. But then, of course, he would be dead too.

He should turn the television on again, but it frightened him. The programmes were for regulars and only reminded him that he, a special, could not emigrate if he wanted to. Why listen to that? he thought crossly. I hope there's a war up there too, and everyone who's emigrated becomes a special.

Right, he thought; time for work. He opened the door and looked out into the unlit hall. Once again, he felt the emptiness of the rest of the building. He was not ready to climb up to the empty roof where he had no animal. He closed the door again and crossed the room to his black empathy box. He turned it on, held the two handles and breathed deeply. The light came on and a picture began to form on the screen. There on a dry, brown hillside under a dark sunless sky was an old man in thin, loose clothes and no shoes. The man, Wilbur Mercer, was walking slowly up the hill and, as he held the handles, John Isidore found himself entering the picture. His own feet now walked across the stones. He felt the familiar roughness under his feet and smelled the bitter air of the sky – not the Earth's sky, but the sky of some distant place. A place that he could always reach through the empathy box.

Like everyone else who at this moment was holding the handles, he was one with Wilbur Mercer and with all those other people on Earth and on other planets. Together they concentrated on the hill, the need to climb. It was impossible to see the end, but one day it would come.

A rock, thrown at him – Wilbur Mercer, the others – hit his arm. He felt the pain. Another rock flew past, missing him. Who was it? He turned to look, but could not see his attackers. As they always did, they had followed him up the hill. He stood, rested, and rubbed the cut on his arm. Why am I up here alone like this with my pain, he thought. Then, inside himself, he could hear the others. They felt the pain too and they walked with him. He was not alone.

Once, he remembered, life had been different. Childhood had been nice; he had loved all life, especially the animals. He

Isidore stood holding the two handles,
experiencing himself and every living thing.

had in fact been able for a time to bring dead animals back to life. Then the killers came and arrested him in his sixteenth year. They said it was now against the law to make dead creatures live again. They attacked his brain with something radioactive and he dropped into a different world full of dead animals and bones. He became part of those dead animals and could not escape until they all started to grow again. In the end it happened and, together, they all began to climb. Then he was walking alone, but the others were there somewhere. He could feel them.

Isidore stood holding the two handles, experiencing himself and every living thing. Then he let go. It had to end, as always, and anyway his arm was hurting. He went slowly to the bathroom to wash the cut. Some people, especially older people, died when they were hit by the rocks. In the city centre there were doctors that you could call, but not out in the suburbs. He dried his arm and heard, far away, the sound of a television.

It's someone else in the building, he thought, unable to believe it. Two or three levels below, in one of the other apartments. Now I'm not alone here. What do you do when a new neighbour moves in? Go and borrow something? He could not remember. People moved away, people emigrated, but nobody ever moved in. You take them something, he decided. Like a cup of milk or maybe an egg – or, to be strictly correct, what people now ate instead of milk and eggs. In his fridge he found a small piece of false butter.

His heart was beating fast as he left his apartment and followed the sound. I mustn't show that I'm a chickenhead, he thought. If he knows I'm a chickenhead, he won't talk to me. It's always the same. Isidore hurried along the hall.

Walking down the dusty stairs, Isidore recognized the familiar voice of Buster Friendly on the television.

' . . . and the dust will be particularly bad in the middle of the day, so if you're thinking of going out, wait until the afternoon. And speaking of waiting, it's now only ten hours until that big piece of news, my special report. Tell your friends to watch! It's something that will really surprise you . . .'

As Isidore knocked on the apartment door, the television fell silent. He could feel the presence of life behind the closed door, and the fear of someone who did not want to see him.

'Hey,' he called. 'I live upstairs. I heard your television. Let's meet.' He waited and listened. No sound and no movement. 'I brought you some butter,' he said. 'My name's J.R. Isidore and I work for the animal doctor Mr Hannibal Sloat. I have a responsible job.'

The door opened a little and he saw a girl. She looked frightened, ill and very weak. She tried to smile.

'You thought this building was empty,' he said as he realized.

'Yes,' the girl whispered.

'But,' Isidore said, 'it's good to have neighbours. I didn't have any until you came.'

'You're the only one here except me?' She seemed less shy now. He saw that she had a nice figure and pretty eyes. Behind her in the room were open suitcases; there were things all over the floor.

'I'm your only neighbour,' Isidore said. 'And I won't bother you.' He felt sad. She was confused, he knew, and she didn't seem to understand about the butter. 'Good old Buster,' he said, trying to make conversation. 'You like him? I watch him every morning and then again after work until I go to bed. Or

I did until my television broke. Now I can only get one station.'

'Who . . .?' the girl began and then stopped and bit her lip.

'Buster Friendly,' he explained. It was odd that she didn't know about him. 'Where have you come here from?' he asked curiously.

'It's not important,' she said quickly. She looked at him carefully and seemed to like what she saw. 'I'd like to talk to you,' she continued, 'but later, when I've organized the apartment. Not now.'

'Why not now?' He did not understand. Everything about her was strange to him. Maybe I've been living here alone too long, he thought. I really am a chickenhead. 'I can look in the other apartments and find you some furniture,' he offered.

'I'll do it,' the girl said. 'Alone.'

'You want to go into those empty apartments alone?' He could not believe it.

'Why not?' Again, she looked uncomfortable; she knew that she had said something wrong.

'The whole building is full of rubbish that people left when they died or emigrated. As you sleep, the rubbish grows and grows.'

'I see,' said the girl uncertainly.

'In the end it will be everywhere. We can't win.'

'Why not?' she asked.

'Nobody can win against rubbish,' he answered. 'In my apartment the situation is under control, but if I die or go away, the rubbish will cover it again. The whole world is moving that way. Except, of course, for the climb of Wilbur Mercer.'

The girl eyed him. 'I don't see the connection.'

'That's what Mercerism is all about,' he said, surprised. 'Don't you have an empathy box?'

After a pause, the girl said carefully, 'I didn't bring mine with me. I thought there'd be one here.'

'But an empathy box,' he cried, 'is so personal! It's a part of yourself. It's the way you touch other human beings so that you're not alone. But you know that. Everyone knows that. Mercer even lets people like me . . .' He stopped, but it was too late. He saw the expression of dislike on her face. She knew. 'I almost passed the intelligence test,' he said in a low voice. 'I'm not *very* special, not like some people. But Mercer doesn't care about that.'

'To me, that's a problem with Mercerism,' the girl said clearly.

'I guess I'll go back upstairs,' he said, turning away from her. The butter was melting in his hand.

The girl watched him go and then called, 'Wait!'

He turned back towards her. 'Why?' he asked.

'I'll need your help with the furniture. What time do you get home from work? You can help me then.'

'Did you get my name?' he said eagerly. 'John Isidore, and I work for . . .'

' . . . some person with the unlikely name of Hannibal Sloat, who is probably only real in your mind.' She looked at him coldly. 'My name is Pris Stratton. You can call me Pris.' She thought for a moment. 'No, call me Miss Stratton. Because we don't really know each other. At least, I don't know you.' She shut the door and he found himself alone in the hall.

I'll make dinner for both of us this evening, Isidore decided

26

as he walked back to his apartment. Maybe she'll change her mind and let me call her Pris.

She's strange, he thought, while he put on his white work uniform; he was going to be late, but that didn't matter. She's never heard of Buster Friendly, and that's impossible. Buster's the most important person alive – except Wilbur Mercer, but Mercer isn't a human being. She may need help. Can I help her? he asked himself. A special, a chickenhead: what do I know? I can't marry and I can't emigrate and in the end the dust will kill me. I have nothing to offer. He went up to the roof and climbed into his old hovercar.

An hour later he collected an electric cat which was not working properly, and drove it in his truck towards the Van Ness Pet Hospital. The cat was making all the right noises for a sick animal; it almost seemed real.

Wow, Isidore said to himself, it's in a bad way. He stopped the truck on a roof and searched the animal for its control box. He could not find it, and while he was looking the cat stopped moving. The owner hasn't been looking after it properly, Isidore thought. It'll be expensive to repair it now. He continued his flight back to the repair shop.

For company, he turned on the radio and listened to Buster Friendly. Like the television programme, Buster's radio broadcast was on twenty-three hours a day. He was interviewing one of those beautiful women who did not sing or act; they were famous only as guests of Buster Friendly. How did Buster manage to make both his television and radio programmes? Isidore wondered. And how did the women always find something new to say?

One thing about Buster worried Isidore. He sometimes made

fun of empathy boxes. He was doing it now.

'And if I'm going up the side of a mountain,' he was saying to his guest, 'I want a couple of bottles of beer with me!'

John Isidore felt angry. Why did Buster's remarks not worry other people? Even the United Nations supported his broadcasts. Maybe Buster is jealous of Wilbur Mercer, Isidore thought. Perhaps they're competing. But for what?

Our minds, Isidore decided. I'll have to tell Hannibal Sloat. Ask him if it's true; he'll know.

Isidore parked his truck on the roof of the hospital and carried the cat downstairs to Hannibal Sloat's office. Mr Sloat was not a special but was too old to emigrate. The dust had made his face grey and he walked with great difficulty. He never cleaned his glasses, so he saw the world through a thick coat of dust.

'What do you have there?' Mr Sloat asked.

'A cat with an electrical problem.'

Mr Sloat took the cat from him. Isidore continued, 'I think Buster Friendly and Mercerism are fighting for control of us.'

'If so,' Sloat answered, examining the cat, 'Buster's winning.'

'He's winning now,' Isidore said, 'but he'll lose in the end.'

Mr Sloat lifted his head. 'Why?'

'Because Wilbur Mercer is for ever. He never dies. At the top of the hill he's wounded and falls, but he always rises again. And we rise with him.' Isidore felt good. He did not usually speak to Mr Sloat so easily.

Sloat said, 'Buster is like Mercer. He won't ever die.'

'That can't be right. He's a man.'

'I don't know,' Sloat said. 'But it's true. They've never admitted it, of course . . . This cat isn't false! I knew that one day this would happen. And it's dead.' He stared at the cat's body and shook his head. 'Another living creature is dead, chickenhead. Didn't you notice the difference?'

Mr Sloat had never called him chickenhead before. Not to his face.

'I th-thought,' Isidore managed to say, 'it was a r-really good job. I mean it seemed alive, and . . .'

'Another dead animal,' Mr Stoat repeated sadly.

'Mercer says,' Isidore reminded him, 'that all life returns. We all climb with him, die, . . .'

'Tell that to the owner of the cat,' Mr Sloat said. 'Phone him now.'

'You mean I have to?' Isidore asked. His heart stopped. He hated videophones. 'You always make the calls. I'm ugly, dirty and grey. I feel sick. I think I'm going to die.'

'Do it, chickenhead, or lose your job,' Sloat said angrily.

'I d-don't like the n-name chickenhead. The d-dust has an effect on all of us, n-not just me.' I can't make the call, he thought, and then he remembered. The owner of the cat was at work; he had seen him leave the apartment. 'I g-guess I can call,' he said as he looked for the number.

He dialled, and a woman's face appeared on the screen. 'Yes?' she said.

'M-mrs Pilsen?' Isidore asked, shaking with fear. 'I want to t-talk to you about your c-c-c-cat. It died.'

'Oh, no,' cried the woman.

'We'll get you another one,' Isidore heard himself saying. 'Tell us what you'd like.'

29

'Horace is dead!' Mrs Pilsen said. 'There's only one cat like Horace. When he was little, . . .'

Isidore had an idea. 'Would you like an electric copy of Horace?' he asked. 'An exact copy?'

'Oh, what are you saying?' Mrs Pilsen cried. 'But yes, you're right. We won't tell my husband. He needn't know anything.'

Mr Sloat took the phone from Isidore. 'Are you sure, madam?' he asked. 'The neighbours won't notice, but the owner always does. When you get near a false animal, . . .'

'My husband never really went near Horace because he was afraid of losing him. I looked after him. I think I *would* like a false animal. I don't think my husband could survive Horace's death. That's why, when he was ill, we waited so long before we called you. Too long . . . I knew that before you phoned. How long will it take?'

'Ten days. We'll deliver it while your husband's at work.' Mr Sloat said goodbye and hung up. He looked at Isidore. 'Not bad,' he said. 'Perhaps you're not so stupid really.'

'I'll take the cat to be measured and photographed,' Isidore said. He felt very, very happy.

4

The chase begins

Rick Deckard parked his police hovercar on the station roof and went down to Inspector Bryant's office.

'That was quick,' his boss said, putting his papers down.

'The trip was a success.' He was tired, Rick realized, and the job ahead of him would be hard. 'How's Dave?' he asked. 'I'd like to talk to him before I go after the first of the androids.'

'You must find Polokov first. The one who shot Dave,' Bryant said. 'He knows we're looking for him.'

'Before I speak to Dave?'

Bryant reached for a sheet of paper. 'Polokov has taken a job with the city as a rubbish collector.'

'Don't only specials do that kind of work?'

'Polokov is pretending to be a special, a chickenhead. That's what gave Dave problems. Polokov's a very good actor. Are you sure about the Voigt-Kampff test now? You're certain, after Seattle, that . . .'

'I am,' Rick said shortly. He did not explain.

'OK,' said Bryant. 'But we can't afford a single mistake.'

'I already found my first Nexus-6,' Rick told him. 'And Dave found two. Three, if you count Polokov. I'll kill Polokov today, and then maybe tonight or tomorrow talk to Dave.' He took the sheet with the information about Polokov from Bryant.

'One more thing,' said Bryant. 'A Russian policeman is on his way here. I had a call from him while you were in Seattle. Sandor Kadalyi, his name is.'

'What does he want?'

'The Russians are also interested in the new Nexus-6 types. They want their man with you to watch – and to help, if he can. I agreed. You won't have to share the money, though,' Bryant added, noticing Rick's expression.

Rick studied the description of Polokov and noted his address and place of work.

'Do you want to wait for the Russian before you go after the android?' Bryant asked. 'He's coming by Aeroflot rocket and it lands soon.'

'I work alone,' Rick answered shortly. 'I'll start now and Kadalyi can find me.'

'OK. And after Polokov, the next android is a Miss Luba Luft. Here's the sheet on her.'

Rick left Bryant's office and returned to his hovercar. Here I come, Polokov, he thought, and he ran his fingers over his laser gun.

His first stop was the company where Polokov worked. It was a large, modern building – you could become very rich these days by collecting rubbish. An official there checked the timetables.

'Polokov should be at work,' he said, after he had looked through them for a moment. He made a call to someone in the building, and then turned back to Rick. 'Polokov didn't come to work this morning. No explanation. What's he done, officer?'

'If he comes in,' Rick said, 'don't tell him I was asking about him. Do you understand?'

'Of course I understand,' the official answered coldly. 'I do know a little about police work.'

Next Rick flew to Polokov's apartment building. Bryant and Holden waited too long, he thought to himself. I should have looked for him last night as soon as Dave was hit.

It was a dark, dirty building. He found Polokov's floor and used his police torch to look again at his information sheet. The Voigt-Kampff test had been given to Polokov, so Rick could forget that part and kill him on sight.

From out here, he decided. He took out his mood weapon, protected himself carefully and turned it on. The weapon sent out electrical waves that prevented everyone in the area, human beings and androids, from moving even a finger. He used a special key to open the apartment door and walked in with his torch in his hand.

No Polokov. Only broken furniture and dust; nothing personal at all. I knew it, Rick said to himself. He's probably left San Francisco. Someone else is going to earn those thousand dollars now. So . . . on to Luba Luft.

Back on the roof in his hovercar, he reported by phone to Inspector Bryant.

'Polokov has escaped. Do you want me to pick up Kadalyi at the field before I look for Luba Luft?'

'He's already here. His rocket arrived early,' Bryant said. 'Just a moment.' There was a pause. 'He'll go and meet you now. Stay where you are.'

While he waited, Rick read about Luba Luft. She was an opera singer working for the San Francisco Opera Company.

She had told the company she was from Germany. She must have a good voice to make connections so fast, he thought. I'll pretend to be an opera lover. We can talk about music while I prepare the test instruments.

The car phone rang. Rick answered, and Rachael Rosen's face appeared. 'Hello, Officer Deckard.' Her voice was friendly. 'Are you busy or can I talk to you?'

'I have a little time.'

'We've been discussing your situation here at the corporation. Since we know the Nexus-6 types well, we think one of us should help you trap them.'

'How?'

'By coming with you. You'll have more success if another Nexus-6 contacts them.'

'You?'

'Yes.' Her expression was serious.

'I've got too much help already. I'll think about it and call you.' At some distant future time, he thought. Probably never.

'You won't call me,' Rachael said. 'We feel we should help because of – you know. What we did.'

'No, thank you.' Rick started to put the phone down.

'Without me,' Rachael said, 'one of them will kill you before you can kill it.'

'Goodbye,' Rick said and hung up. An android offering him her help! What kind of world was this?

A hovercar taxi landed on the roof. A man with a red face in his mid-fifties and wearing a big Russian coat climbed out. He smiled at Rick and walked across to his car as the taxi left.

'Mr Deckard?' the man said, with a strong accent. 'I'm Sandor Kadalyi.' He opened the door to Rick's car and got in

34

'*I got it on Mars. Try it.*'

beside him. They shook hands and Rick noticed that he carried a strange kind of laser gun.

Kadalyi's eyes followed his. 'This?' Kadalyi asked, showing it to him. 'Interesting, isn't it? I got it on Mars. Try it.'

Rick pointed it out of the window and fired. Nothing.

'You need this,' Kadalyi said, laughing, and opened his hand. There was a small piece of metal in it. 'You fire with

35

this, and it doesn't matter what the gun is aimed at.'

'You're not a Russian policeman, you're Polokov,' Rick suddenly realized. With his foot he touched the emergency button on the floor of his car.

'My laser's not firing,' Kadalyi-Polokov said angrily.

'I've got equipment in this car,' Rick said, 'that breaks up the laser beam and spreads it out into ordinary light.'

'Then I'll have to break your neck,' the android replied and threw himself at Rick.

As the android's hands held his throat, Rick fired an old-style gun from its place under his arm. The bullet hit the android in the head and the android's brain box burst. The Nexus-6 controls blew into pieces which fell on Rick. He shook them off and, shakily, reached for the car phone.

'Tell Bryant that I got Polokov,' he said to the officer who answered. 'He'll understand.' He breathed deeply. It almost killed me, he thought. Slowly his heart returned to its normal speed, but he was still shaking. A thousand dollars, he thought. And I reacted faster than Dave. Of course his experience prepared me. Dave had no warning.

Rick lit a cigarette, then picked up the phone again and rang his home number. He saw his wife's miserable face in front of him.

'Oh hello, Rick.'

'What happened to the 594 mood that I dialled for you?'

'I redialled. What do you want? I'm so tired and I have no hope, none at all. Our marriage is terrible, and you'll be killed by one of those androids, and . . .'

'Listen,' he said impatiently. 'I'm investigating a new kind of android that nobody can trap except me. I've killed one, so that's a good start. Do you know what we're going to have when I finish?'

'Yes,' Iran answered. Her eyes were dull and expressionless.

'I haven't told you yet!' He could see that she was too depressed to listen to him. 'I'll see you tonight,' he finished bitterly, and hung up. Why do I risk my life? he asked himself. She doesn't care about ostriches. We should go our own ways. Most androids have a stronger wish to live than my wife.

He thought about Rachael Rosen again. Maybe I *could* use her if she doesn't want any of the money. He started his hovercar and set out for the opera house. He wondered now about Rachael; some androids seemed very pretty. It was a strange feeling, reacting to a machine like that. She's too thin, he decided. Like a child. How old is Luba Luft? He looked in his notes for her 'age'. Twenty-eight – in appearance.

I'll try one more android before I ask Rachael for help, Rick decided. If Miss Luft is really hard – but I think Polokov was probably the hardest. The others don't know I'm coming for them.

As he landed on the roof of the opera house, he was singing loudly. He had no mood machine in the car, but he was happy again. And ready.

The singers were rehearsing and he recognized the music he loved Mozart. It took longer, though, before he recognized the woman in front of him as Luba Luft. His third Nexus-6 android. She sang, and her voice was fantastic, one of the best that he had ever heard. The Rosen Corporation built her well, he admitted to himself. But then the better she sings, the more I'm needed.

There was no problem until the quality of androids became so high.

The practice ended. Rick followed the last singers to the dressing-rooms and found a door with MISS LUFT PRIVATE on it. He knocked.

'Come in!'

He entered. The girl was studying her sheets of music and using a pen to make notes on them.

'Yes?' she said, looking up. 'I am busy, as you can see.' Her English was completely without accent.

'You're an excellent singer,' Rick said.

'Who are you?' Her voice was cold, like the voices of many androids.

'I'm from the San Francisco Police,' he told her.

'Oh?' There was no reaction in her eyes. 'What do you want?'

'I've been sent here to give you a test.'

'An intelligence test?'

'No. Empathy.'

'I'll have to put on my glasses.' She started to look for them.

'If you can make notes on your music without your glasses, you can do the test without them. I'll show you some pictures and ask you some questions.' Rick prepared his instruments, attached the wires to her face and shone a light in her eyes. 'That's it,' he told her.

'Do you think I'm an android? I'm not. I've never been to Mars. I've never even seen an android!' She was trying to stay calm. 'Have you got information about an android here in the opera house? I'll help you. If I were an android, would I help you?'

'An android,' Rick answered, 'doesn't care about other

androids. That's one of the signs we look for.'

'Then,' Miss Luft said, '*you* must be an android.'

This stopped him; he stared at her.

'Because,' she continued, 'your job is to kill them, isn't it? This test you want to give me . . .' Her voice was growing stronger. 'Have you taken it?'

'Yes. A long time ago. When I first worked for the police.'

'Maybe that's a false memory. Don't androids sometimes have false memories? I'll take the test if *you* take it first.'

He stared at her again, and then shook his head. 'You need experience to give the Voigt-Kampff test. Now please listen carefully. I'm going to describe situations to you. I want you to tell me what you'd do in those situations. And I want you to answer quickly. The speed of your reaction is important.'

He chose his first question. 'You are watching an old film on television, a film from before the war. It shows a meal. The main dish is boiled dog with rice.'

'Nobody kills and eats dogs,' Luba Luft said. 'They're too expensive. You mean a false dog. But those are made of wires and motors. You can't *eat* them.'

'Before the war,' Rick said crossly.

'I wasn't alive before the war.'

'But you've s____ ____ _l__ fil__ ____ ___ ____ _____

'Because they ate dog with rice in the Philippines. I remember that.'

'But your reaction,' he said. 'I want your reaction.'

'To the film?' She thought about it. 'I'd turn it off and watch Buster Friendly.'

'Why would you turn it off?'

'Well,' she answered. 'Who wants to watch an old film about the Philippines?' She looked at him angrily. The needles were moving violently, but after a conversation like that the movements were meaningless.

He paused, then said. 'You rent a little house in the mountains.'

'OK.'

'Above the fireplace is a deer's head . . .'

'What's a deer?'

'It's an animal that used to live in the woods. People killed them for sport.'

'Tell me the German word.'

He couldn't remember it. 'Your English is perfect,' he said angrily.

'My *accent* is perfect. It has to be for the singing. But there are many words I don't know.'

He did not know whether she was acting or not. He decided to try another question. 'A man invites you to his apartment. While you're there . . .'

'Oh no,' Luba said quickly, 'I wouldn't be there. That's easy to answer.'

'That's not the question!'

'Did you read the wrong question?' She rubbed her face and the wires fell to the floor.

'I'll get them,' Rick said. When he stood up again, a laser gun was pointing at him.

'Questions about men's apartments,' said Luba Luft confidently, 'are not very nice. You're not from the police.'

'You can see my card,' he said, putting his hand in his

pocket. He was shaking again, he noticed.

'If you remove that hand from your pocket,' Luba Luft said, 'I'll kill you.' She picked up her videophone and dialled a number. 'Connect me to the San Francisco Police Station,' she ordered. 'I need a policeman.'

'That's very sensible of you,' Rick said when she hung up. But it was strange. Why didn't she kill him? She couldn't do it after the officer arrived.

A few minutes later a large man in police uniform entered the room.

'All right,' he said to Luba Luft. 'Put that gun down.' Then he turned to Rick. 'Who are you?' he asked.

Luba Luft said, 'He came in here and wanted to ask me questions – very rude, personal questions to ask a woman.'

'Show me your card,' the officer said to Rick.

Rick gave it to him. 'I'm an android killer,' he explained. 'I work for Inspector Harry Bryant. I'm working with Dave Holden's list now he's in hospital.'

'I know all the android killers and I've never heard of you,' the police officer said. 'Or Inspector Bryant.' Rick realized what was happening.

'You're an android,' he told the man. 'Like Miss Luft.' He walked towards the phone. 'Let me talk to Inspector Bryant.'

There was a pause after he dialled, and then Bryant's face appeared. Rick explained the problem.

'Let me talk to the officer,' Bryant said. Rick held out the phone to the police officer.

'Officer Crams . . . Hello?' The man listened for a moment

and then turned to Rick. 'There's nobody there.' Rick looked at the video screen. Nothing. 'I'm going to take you to the police station and question you there,' Crams continued.

'OK,' Rick said. And, to Luba Luft, 'I haven't finished testing you yet. I'll be back soon.'

Officer Crams searched Rick and took his guns. He smelt the old one. 'This has just been fired,' he said.

'I killed an android. The pieces are in my car.'

'We'll go up and have a look then.'

'Don't let him come near me again, officer,' Luba Luft said as they left. 'He's very strange. I'm afraid of him.'

'If he's got a dead body in the car, he won't return,' Crams told her. He pushed Rick and they went up to the roof. Crams opened the door to Rick's hovercar and looked silently at the pieces of Polokov.

'An android,' Rick said. 'I was sent to find it. It almost killed me when it pretended to be . . .'

'Wait until we arrive at the police station.' He led Rick to the police car, and they climbed in.

Something, Rick noticed after a moment, was not right. They were going the wrong way.

'The police station,' he said, 'is north on Lombard.'

'That's the old one,' Officer Crams said. 'It's just dust now. Nobody uses it. The new one is on Mission.'

'Take me to the old one,' Rick said. He understood now what the two androids, working together, had done. This was probably his last ride.

'That girl's very pretty,' Officer Crams said.

'Tell me that you're an android,' said Rick.

'Why? I'm not an android. What do you do? Kill people

42

and tell yourself they're android. You're dangerous. I agree with Miss Luft. Maybe you're an android with a false memory. Have you thought of that?' Crams smiled.

Rick knew there was nothing he could say. He sat and waited. The androids had trapped him now. But I did get one of them, he told himself. And Dave got two.

Officer Crams' police car prepared to land.

5

On trial

The Mission Street police station was an exciting modern building. Rick Deckard liked it – except for one thing. He had never seen it before.

'304,' Officer Crams said to the man on the front desk, 'and 612.4. And pretending to work for the police.'

'That's 406.7,' the other man said, and completed the necessary papers.

'Over here,' Officer Crams said to Rick, leading him to a small white table full of equipment. 'Head measurements for identification purposes.'

'I know,' Rick said crossly. In the old days, when he had been a young officer himself, he had brought many people to a table like this. *Like* this, but not this particular table.

Next, in another room, his clothes were searched and everything he had was listed. It makes no sense, he thought. Who are these people? If this place has always existed, why didn't we know about it? Two police organizations, ours and this one, but no contact between them . . . until now. Or perhaps this isn't the first time. And perhaps these aren't really police officers.

A man, not in uniform, approached Rick slowly and looked at him curiously. 'What's this one?' he asked Officer Crams.

44

'Suspected murder,' Crams answered. 'There's a body in his car – but he says it's an android. We're checking that now, doing bone tests on the body. And pretending to be a police officer, an android killer, to enter a woman's dressing-room and ask her offensive questions. She called us. Do you wish to interview him, sir?'

'All right.' Crams' boss looked at Rick again, then took his bag. 'What do you have in here, Mr Deckard?'

'Material for the Voigt-Kampff empathy test,' Rick said. 'I was testing a suspect when Officer Crams arrested me.' The officer was searching his bag and examining everything in it. 'I asked Miss Luft the normal V-K questions . . .'

'Do you know George Gleason and Phil Resch?'

'No,' Rick answered. The names meant nothing to him.

'They're the android killers for Northern California. They work here. Are you an android, Mr Deckard? From time to time we have escaped androids here pretending to be android killers chasing a suspect.'

'I'm not an android. You can give me the Voigt-Kampff test. I've taken it before and I know what the results will be. Can I phone my wife?'

'You can make one call. Do you want to phone her or a lawyer?'

'My wife can get a lawyer . . .'

. . . appeared, but it was not from . . . He hung up.

'No luck?' said the officer. 'Well, you can try again later. I can't let you go, though, because your crimes are very serious. Come into my office. I'd like to talk to you.'

'My name's Garland,' the man said, when they were both sitting down. 'Is this Voigt-Kampff test efficient?'

'It's the only one we use. Don't you know it?' Rick asked.

'No,' Garland said. He paused. 'This list from your bag – Polokov, Miss Luft . . . The next name on it is me.'

Rick stared at him and then took the paper. Neither of them spoke for a moment.

'It's very unpleasant,' Garland said, 'to find yourself on a list like this. I've asked Phil Resch to join us. I want to see *his* list.'

'Do you think I'm on it?' Rick asked.

'It's possible. This description of me is correct except for my job. Yes, it's certainly me.'

The office door opened and a tall man with a beard and glasses came in. Garland explained everything to him.

'I talked to Polokov once,' Phil Resch said. 'Very cold. I wanted to test him too.' He turned to Rick. 'Have you tested Inspector Garland?'

'Of course not!' Garland said.

'I've always said,' Resch continued, 'that the best place for an android would be in a big police station.'

Garland opened his mouth to speak, but the videophone rang. It was Garland's secretary.

'Inspector Garland, we have the results of the tests on Mr Polokov's body. Mr Polokov was a humanlike android.'

Garland looked at the far wall; he said nothing to Rick or Phil Resch.

'So yours is an empathy test, Mr Deckard,' Resch said to Rick. 'Ours is probably simpler. We play a noise or show a light and the suspect pushes a button. We measure the time of the reaction. Then we can do the bone tests, as we did with Polokov, to be sure.'

Rick was silent. Then he said, 'You can test me. I'm ready. But I'd like to test you too, if that's all right with you.'

'Of course,' Resch said. 'They should test higher officers more often too.' He looked at Garland.

Garland smiled at him. 'You're not going to like the results of your test,' he said.

Resch did not look pleased. 'I'll get the Boneli instruments,' he said to Rick, and left the office.

Garland looked in his desk drawer, took out a laser gun, and pointed it at Rick.

'Why?' Rick asked. 'They'll test my body and they'll know that I wasn't an android. You can't win.'

Garland stared at him, then put the gun down again. 'Resch is an android too,' he said. 'He doesn't suspect, though. I came with the others on a ship from Mars. Not Resch – he stayed another week and was given a false memory. When he learns the truth, he'll probably kill all of us. That's what happens, I understand, when an android thought he was human.'

'So why do you put these false memories in if it's so dangerous?' Rick asked.

'It's all a risk,' Garland said. 'Coming here to Earth where we're less impo~~rtant~~.'

abou~~t~~

had any c~~ome~~ ~~our~~ group. I took a chance on the test. So did Crams.'

'When I phoned my wife,' Rick said, 'why didn't I get her?'

'If you call from here, you reach another office in the same building. We're separate from the rest of San Francisco. We know about them, but they don't know about us. Sometimes we bring someone like you in, for our own protection.' There were footsteps in the hall. 'Here comes Resch now. Isn't he clever? He's going to kill us both.'

'You androids don't help each other at difficult times,' Rick said.

'No,' Garland agreed sharply. 'We don't have, do we, that special thing that you humans have. I believe it's called empathy.'

The office door opened. Phil Resch came in carrying a machine with a number of different wires hanging from it.

'Here we are,' he said, and sat down.

Garland suddenly raised his right hand. Resch and Rick rolled on to the floor. At the same time, Resch pulled out his laser gun and fired at Garland. The beam hit Garland in the head. His body fell forwards and then dropped off the chair.

'It forgot,' Resch said as he stood up again, 'that this is my job. I always know what an android's going to do.' He looked at the body. 'What did it say to you while I wasn't here?'

'That he – it – was an android. And you . . .' Rick paused, and then changed his mind. 'And you would kill it.'

'What else?'

'This building is full of androids.'

Resch thought for a moment. 'Then we're going to have trouble getting out of here,' he said. 'Usually, of course, I can leave when I want. And take a prisoner with me.' He listened. There was silence outside the office. 'I guess nobody heard.' He picked up the videophone. 'Inspector Garland is busy for the next half an hour,' he said into it. 'He doesn't want to be disturbed.'

'Yes, Mr Resch,' a voice answered.

'Let's go,' Resch said to Rick. 'And remember that you're under arrest until we're outside the building.'

They walked past the uniformed guards and travelled up to the roof.

'Do you think your station will give me a job?' Resch asked. 'I think I've lost mine now.'

Rick hesitated. 'I – I don't see why not. But we already have two android killers.' I've got to tell him that he's an android, he thought. He got me out of that place, but he's everything that we both hate.

'Why didn't I know they were androids?' Phil Resch asked. 'I've been working for them for three years.'

'Garland and his friends only came to Earth a few months ago,' Rick told him.

'Then there was once a real Garland. Or – I've got a false memory system.' His face turned grey. 'Only androids have false memory systems. Those systems don't work in human beings.'

They were up on the roof now.

'Here's my car,' Resch said and waved Rick inside. They lifted into the sky and drove north in the direction of the Opera House. Resch's mind was not on the journey.

'Listen, Deckard,' he said suddenly. 'After we kill Luba Luft, I want you to . . . you know . . . give me the Boneli test or that empathy test. I need to know.'

'We can worry about that later,' Rick answered slowly.

'You don't want me to take it, do you?' Resch looked at

him. 'Garland told you something about me.'

'Let's just concentrate on Luba Luft. That's going to be hard.'

'It's not just false memory systems,' Phil Resch said. 'I own an animal; not a false one, but the real thing. A squirrel. Its name's Buffy. I love that squirrel, Deckard. Every morning I feed it and then in the evening I bring it into my apartment and it plays there. It has a wheel and it runs inside that too. It runs and runs, the wheel turns, but Buffy stays in the same place.'

'I guess squirrels aren't very intelligent,' Rick said.

They flew on in silence.

At the opera house, they were told that the rehearsal had finished and Miss Luft had left. Resch showed his identification.

'Do you know where she went?' he asked.

'To the museum. She wanted to see the Edvard Munch paintings.'

'Did you ever hear of an android with a pet?' Resch asked as they walked to the museum.

Rick decided to be honest. 'I know of two cases,' he answered, 'but it isn't common. The android usually can't keep the animal alive. Animals need love.'

'Would a squirrel need that? Love? Buffy's happy and healthy.'

They were inside the museum now, and Resch stopped in front of a painting. It showed a hairless creature standing alone on a bridge. Its hands were held over its ears in horror and its mouth was open in a soundless scream.

'I think,' Phil Resch said, 'that this is how an android must feel. I don't feel like that, so maybe I'm not an . . .' He stopped as other people came near them.

'There's Luba Luft.' Rick pointed, and they walked quietly towards her. They did not want to frighten other museum visitors.

Luba Luft was looking at a drawing of a young girl sitting on the edge of a bed.

'Do you want me to buy it for you?' Rick asked Luba Luft,

'Do you want me to buy it for you?'

gently taking her arm. On the other side of her, Phil Resch put his hand on her shoulder and Rick saw the end of his laser gun.

'It's not for sale.' Luba Luft looked at Rick and the colour left her face. 'I thought they arrested you.'

'Miss Luft,' he said, 'this is Mr Resch. The officer that arrested me is an android. So was his boss. Do you know – did you know – an Inspector Garland? He told me you all came here on the same ship.'

'The police station that you called,' Phil Resch added, 'seems to be an organization through which your group keeps in touch. They even feel confident enough to hire a human being as an android killer . . .'

'You?' Luba Luft said. 'You're not a human being. You're an android, like me.'

There was a silence, then Resch said to Rick in a low voice, 'Let's take her to my car.'

Luba Luft seemed to accept the situation. She went quietly, but stopped beside the museum shop. 'Listen,' she said to Rick. Some colour had returned to her face. 'Buy me a copy of that painting of the girl on the bed.'

After a pause, Rick asked the shop assistant for a copy.

'We only have one in this book,' the assistant told him. 'Twenty-five dollars.'

'I'll take it.' Rick reached for his wallet, bought the book and gave it to Luba Luft. They went into the lift.

'Thank you,' she said. 'No android would do that.' She looked at Phil Resch. '*You* wouldn't. I really don't like androids. Since I came here, I've been pretending to be a human being, acting and thinking as they do. That's how it is, isn't it Resch? Trying to be . . .'

'I can't listen to this,' Resch said, and reached for his gun.

'No,' Rick said. 'The test.'

'We don't have to wait. It said it's an android.'

'But you mustn't kill it because it annoys you.' He tried to take the gun from Resch, but could not.

Phil Resch fired. Luba Luft, terror on her face, jumped sideways, but the beam hit her in the stomach. She stared in front of her and screamed. Like the picture, Rick thought, and killed her with his own laser gun.

'I'm leaving this business,' he told Resch. 'I'll emigrate and go to Mars.'

'Someone has to do it,' Phil Resch replied.

'They can use androids. I've had enough. She was a wonderful singer and she liked paintings. The planet could have used her. This is crazy.'

'This is necessary. Remember that they killed humans before they escaped. And they wanted to kill *you* in that police station. Didn't Polokov almost kill you? *They're* attacking *us*. They're pretending to be . . .'

'Police,' Rick continued, 'android killers.'

'Maybe Garland lied about me. What about my squirrel?'

'Yes, I forgot about your squirrel.' They were on the first floor now and the doors opened. People were looking at them. 'You stay here with the body, and I'll phone for a police car.'

He found a phone and called. How can such a beautiful voice be so dangerous? he thought as he hung up. But it wasn't the voice – it was the android itself. I can't leave the job now.

Rick returned to Phil Resch. 'I hope you *are* an android,' he said. 'The way you killed Garland and then Luba Luft – you don't kill like I do. You enjoy it. If you fail your test, will you kill yourself?' Androids rarely did that.

'Yes,' Phil Resch answered. 'You only have to test me. I'll do the rest.'

A police car arrived and took the body away. Rick and Resch walked back to the opera house in silence, and travelled up to the roof. They climbed into the hovercar. 'Here's my laser gun,' Phil Resch said. 'You'll tell me the truth, won't you?'

'Sure.' Rick took out his instruments and explained the test. 'Here's the first question.' The test began.

Afterwards, Rick did not speak. He felt very tired.

'I can tell by your face,' Resch said, breathing deeply. 'You can give me my gun back.'

'Garland was lying to make us suspect each other,' Rick answered slowly. 'But you have got one problem. One that we don't test for. Your feelings towards androids.'

'We can't test for that,' Phil Resch said quietly. 'Empathy towards animals is one thing. If we felt empathy towards androids too . . .'

'We wouldn't be able to protect ourselves.' Rick finished the sentence. Then he looked at Resch. 'I want to ask myself a question. Tell me what the needles show. Don't worry about speed of reaction.'

'Sure, Rick,' Resch agreed. Rick showed him the controls.

'I'm going down in a lift with an android that I've caught. And suddenly somebody kills it without warning.'

'No particular reaction,' Resch told him.

'What did the needles hit?'

'The left one 2.8. The right one 3.3.'

Rick said, 'A female android.'

'Now they're up to 4.0 and 6.0.'

'That's high.' Rick removed the wires from his face. 'I'm capable of feeling empathy for at least two particular female androids.' And Luba Luft is one, he thought. There's nothing unnatural about Phil Resch – it's *me*.

Resch seemed amused. 'It's love,' he said. 'Some of them are really pretty. Don't you know that there are people on other planets who sleep with their androids? Your only problem is that you want to go to bed with a female android. I felt like that a couple of times. The answer is to love them *before*, not after, you kill them.'

Rick stared at him. Resch is a good android killer, he said to himself. But am I? Suddenly, for the first time in his life, he was not sure.

6

New arrivals

John R. Isidore drove through the sky on his way home from work. I wonder if she's still there, he asked himself. Watching Buster Friendly on her television and shaking with fear when she hears somebody in the hall.

Including, I suppose, me.

On the seat beside him were some fruit and some very expensive cheese. They had cost two weeks' salary, borrowed from Mr Sloat. And under the seat was a bottle of wine that he had kept in a box at the Bank of America for years. He had always refused to sell it; he was waiting for a girl to arrive in his life. That had never happened, not until now.

He arrived at his apartment building and carried the food and drink carefully downstairs to Pris Stratton's apartment. He knocked.

'Who's there?' Her voice was sharp but frightened.

'This is J.R. Isidore here,' he said with the new confidence that he had had since using Mr Sloat's videophone. 'I've brought some things for dinner.'

The door opened. 'You sound different,' Pris said. 'More adult.' She noticed what he was carrying and her face lit with excitement. Then the excitement disappeared again, and her normal bitter expression returned.

'What is it?' he asked as he put everything down in her kitchen.

'They're wasted on me.'

'Why?'

'Oh . . . One day I'll tell you. It was nice of you, though. Now you must leave. I want to be alone.'

'I know what's the matter with you,' he said. 'You don't have any friends, so you're all alone.'

'I have friends.' Her voice was stronger now. 'Or I had. Seven of them. But the killers are looking for them. Maybe now they're all dead. You could be right. I may have no friends now.'

'Who are these killers?' Isidore asked. He didn't understand. 'Are they trying to kill *you*? It's against Mercerism. Can't you go to the police?'

'No.'

Perhaps she's a special and she's imagining the danger, he thought. 'I'll get them first if they come here,' he offered.

'With what?' She smiled.

'I'll get a permit for a laser. It isn't difficult when you live away from the centre. The police don't often come to these areas.'

'And when you're at work?'

'I'll take a holiday.'

'It's very nice of you, J.R. Isidore,' Pris said. 'But if the killers got the others – got Max Polokov and Garland and Luba and Roy Baty . . . Oh, Roy and Irmgard Baty are my best friends. If they're dead, nothing matters. Why don't I hear from them?'

Isidore went to the kitchen and found some dusty plates

and glasses. He washed them carefully. After he had dried them, he opened the wine and divided the food. Pris sat down and tried some fruit. Then she began to cry. Isidore did not know what to do. Suddenly Pris stood up again.

'We lived on Mars,' she said slowly. 'All of us. It was an awful place. If you think I'm miserable now, well, I was much more unhappy there. And very lonely.'

'Don't the androids keep you company? I heard an advertisement . . .'

She drank a little wine. 'The androids,' she said, 'are lonely too.'

Isidore opened his mouth to speak again, but at that moment there was a knock on the front door. Pris looked at Isidore white-faced.

'We can't open it,' she whispered. 'Don't make any noise!'

A woman's voice called from the hall, 'Pris? Are you in there?' Then a man, 'It's Roy and Irmgard. We got your card.'

Pris stood up and found a pen and paper. She wrote a message and passed it to Isidore. YOU GO TO THE DOOR.

Isidore took her pen nervously and wrote: AND SAY WHAT?

Angrily, Pris replied: SEE IF IT'S REALLY THEM.

Isidore walked slowly into the living room. How will I know if it is them? he asked himself. He opened the door.

Two people stood in the dark hall. One was a small, beautiful woman in fashionable clothes with blue eyes and golden hair. The man had intelligent eyes and a flat face that made him look foreign.

'We're looking . . .' the woman began, but then she looked past Isidore and ran into the apartment calling, 'Pris! How are you?' Isidore turned. The women were in each other's arms. He stood back and Roy Baty followed his wife in. He had an odd, cold smile on his face.

'Can we talk?' Roy said to Pris, and then looked at Isidore.

'More or less,' Pris answered, smiling with happiness. She took the two visitors to one side and whispered for a moment, then she turned back to Isidore, who was starting to feel very uncomfortable.

'This is Mr Isidore,' Pris told her friends. 'He's been looking after me. He brought me some natural food.'

'Food . . .' repeated Irmgard, and went into the kitchen to see. 'Fruit!' She started eating it immediately. Isidore found her warmer than Pris and followed her to the table. 'You're from Mars.'

'Yes,' she answered, and her blue eyes shone at him. 'What an awful building you live in. Nobody else lives here, do they? We didn't see any other lights.'

'I live upstairs,' Isidore explained.

'Oh, I thought perhaps you and Pris were living together.'

Roy and Pris had come into the kitchen after them.

'Well, they got Polokov,' Roy said. Pris's happy smile disappeared.

'Who else?' she asked.

'Anders and Gitchel before that. Garland, and then – a little earlier today – they got Luba.' He sounded pleased that he was shocking Pris.

'So that leaves . . .'

'The three of us,' Irmgard said.

'That's why we're here,' Roy added.

'They had this killer called Dave Holden,' Irmgard explained

59

anxiously. 'Polokov almost got him, and now he's in hospital. He gave his list to another killer and Polokov almost got *him* too. But in the end he killed Polokov. And then he went after Luba. She phoned Garland and Garland sent someone to pick him up. She thought Garland would kill him, but something went wrong on Mission Street. We don't know what.'

'Does this killer have our names?' Pris asked.

'Oh yes, dear, he probably does. But he doesn't know where we are. Roy and I have brought all our things, and we'll move into one of these apartments.'

'Is that a g-good idea?' Isidore suddenly managed to speak. 'T-to be all in one place?'

'It may not make any difference,' Irmgard said. Her voice was strangely flat now, without expression. They're all odd, Isidore thought. Except Pris. She was really frightened – she seemed almost normal. But . . .

'Why don't you move in with him?' Roy asked Pris, pointing to Isidore. 'He could give you some protection.'

'A chickenhead?' Pris said. 'I'm not going to live with a chickenhead.'

'You shouldn't be proud at a time like this,' Irmgard told her, speaking quickly. 'The killers may come tonight.'

'I think you should move in with Isidore, Pris,' Roy agreed. 'And we'll stay here too so we can help each other. I'll put in a listening system so that we can hear what's happening in your apartment, and you can hear us, and I'll also organize some alarms. If he's coming, he'll arrive soon, because that's how they work. If he doesn't come, we'll move somewhere else.'

Isidore spoke: 'I g-gather from l-listening to Mr Baty that he's your natural leader.'

'Oh, yes. He's a leader,' Irmgard said. 'He planned our . . . trip, from Mars to here.'

'Then,' Isidore said, 'you must do what h-he suggests.' His voice was full of hope. 'Pris, if you l-live with me, I'll stay at h-home for a few days. To make sure you're all right.' Unbelievable, he thought, that the police can't do anything. These people must have done something. But nobody kills another human being these days.

'The chickenhead,' Pris said, 'likes me.'

'Don't call him that,' Irmgard said, giving Isidore a warm look. 'Think what he could call *you*.'

'I'll go and get some wires,' Roy said. 'Irmgard and I'll stay in this apartment.' He hurried out of the front door.

'OK, J.R., I'll move in with you and you can protect me,' Pris told him.

Irmgard touched Isidore's arm. 'I want you to know that we're very grateful to you, Mr Isidore. You're the first friend that any of us have found on Earth. I hope that one day we can repay your kindness.'

Isidore led Pris upstairs to his own apartment. He turned on the lights, the heater and the only television station that worked.

'I like this,' Pris said, although her normal bitter expression did not show any pleasure. 'None of it's true, you know. We're all crazy; we took a lot of drugs on Mars and now we imagine things, have group dreams. We don't know what's real and what isn't.'

'I didn't think it was true,' Isidore said happily.

'Why didn't you?' She stared at him.

'B-because the government never kills anyone, for any crime. And Mercerism . . .'

'But if you're not human,' Pris said, 'it's all different.'

'That's not true. Even animals – and birds – are protected by law.'

'Especially insects,' Roy added. He had come in while they were talking. He lifted a picture from the living-room wall, hung a small piece of listening equipment, and covered it again with the picture. 'Now the alarm. These wires go under the carpet. The alarm rings if a – if somebody else steps on them. Not one of us.'

'And when it rings? He'll have a gun,' Pris said.

'This system has a mood machine in it. Unless our visitor acts very fast, he'll feel a great sense of fear. He won't be able to stay here for more than a few seconds before running away. Then we'll catch him.'

'But the alarm will have an effect on Isidore too,' Pris reminded Roy.

'That doesn't matter. They'll both rush out. But Isidore won't start the alarm by himself. It needs another human. And the killer won't attack Isidore; he's not on the list.'

'You're androids,' Isidore realized. 'I see why they want to kill you. Actually, you're not alive.' He understood everything now. The killer, the deaths of their friends, the trip to earth. 'It doesn't matter to me. I'm a special. They're not very nice to me either. I can't emigrate.' He couldn't stop talking now. '*You* can't come here; *I* can't . . .' He calmed himself.

After a pause, Roy Baty said, 'You wouldn't like Mars. You aren't missing anything.'

'We are different, aren't we?' Pris said.

'I wish I had your intelligence,' Isidore said. 'Then I wouldn't be a chickenhead. I could learn a lot from you.'

'You're androids.'

Roy finished his alarm system in silence.

'He doesn't understand,' said Pris in a sharp voice, 'how we got off Mars. What we did there.'

Irmgard spoke. She was standing at the door. 'I don't think we have to worry about Mr Isidore,' she said seriously, looking up into Isidore's face. 'He knows us and he likes us . . . and that's everything to him. It's hard for us to understand that, but it's true.'

'You're a great man, Isidore,' Pris said.

'If he were an android,' Roy added, laughing, 'he'd call the police tomorrow morning on his way to work. But he's going to keep quiet to help us. Isn't that wonderful?' Isidore could not tell if he was sincere or not. 'And we imagined this would be a friendless world.'

'I'm not worried,' Irmgard said.

'You should be,' said Roy.

'Let's vote,' Pris suggested, 'like we did on the ship.'

'Well, I won't say anything more,' said Irmgard, 'but I think Mr Isidore is . . .'

'Special,' Pris said.

Irmgard and Pris voted to stay. Roy voted to kill Isidore and move somewhere else. The females won.

'I'm tired, Isidore,' Roy explained as he accepted defeat. 'It's been a long trip.'

'I hope,' said Isidore happily, 'I can help make your stay on Earth pleasant.' After his recent experience with the videophone, he felt sure he could.

7

A call for help

As soon as he officially finished work that evening, Rick Deckard flew across town to animal row, a street of animal dealers with huge glass windows and bright signs. The depression that had hit him earlier that day had not lifted, but the sight of animals always made him feel better.

'Yes, sir,' a salesman said as he stared at the creatures in one of the shops. 'See anything you like?'

'I like all of them,' Rick replied. 'The problem is the cost. I've got three thousand dollars.' The station had paid him his money for the three androids.

'What about a goat, sir? Three thousand is a good first payment on a goat. The advantage of a goat is that you can teach it to attack thieves. And, unlike other animals, it can eat anything. If a cow or a horse eats something radioactive, it dies. A cat's the same. But not a goat, sir. This one's female – a very beautiful black Nubian female. And the price is good.' The assistant wrote a figure on a piece of paper.

Rick checked his Sydney's. Then he took the piece of paper and wrote a lower figure.

'Oh, no. That's not enough! She's less than a year old.' The assistant wrote again.

'It's a deal,' Rick said, and passed over all his money.

Employees of the animal dealer helped him load the goat into his hovercar. I own an animal now, Rick said to himself. A living animal, not electric. For the second time in my life. The cost frightened him; he found that he was shaking. But I had to do it, he told himself. The experience with Phil Resch – I need to find my confidence again, or I won't keep my job.

He drove off in the direction of his apartment and Iran. She'll be angry, he thought, because we're responsible for this goat now. And she'll have to look after it since she's at home all day. Again he felt depressed. He landed on the roof and lifted the goat out. It looked at him with bright eyes but made no sound. Rick hurried downstairs.

'Hello,' Iran greeted him, busy with the dinner. 'You're late tonight.'

'Come up to the roof,' Rick said. 'I want to show you something.'

'You bought an animal!' She followed him immediately. 'But why did you buy it without me? It's the most important thing we'll ever buy. You made some money, didn't you?'

'Yes. I killed three androids. I had to buy this,' Rick explained. 'Something went wrong today, something about killing them. I need an animal so that I can continue.'

They were outside now, and he pointed silently at the goat.

'Oh, my god!' Iran said softly. 'A black Nubian goat. Is it real?'

'Yes,' Rick replied. 'It's real, and it's female, so perhaps we'll have babies one day. And we can make cheese from her milk.'

Iran put her hand gently on his shoulder and kissed him. 'I love you,' she said.

'Is it real?'

'Thank you,' he said, and kissed her.

Iran pulled at his arm. 'Let's run downstairs and thank Mercer. Then we can come up here again and name her.'

As they walked inside, their neighbour Bill Barbour called to them.

'That's a nice-looking goat you have there, Deckard.

Congratulations. One baby horse for two little goats one day, perhaps?'

'Thank you,' Rick said. 'Does this put an end to your depression?' he asked his wife.

'It certainly does,' she answered. 'Come on. We must share this mood with everyone.'

She was right, of course, although she experienced this sharing more easily than he did. When they reached their living room, they turned on the empathy box. The screen showed streams of colours and Iran reached for the handles.

'Listen, Iran,' Rick said urgently, pulling her away from the box, 'I need to talk about what happened today. I met another killer; one who seemed to enjoy killing. For the first time, after being with him, I began to empathize with the androids. Like you did this morning. That's why I bought the goat. Maybe it was a depression. I never understood yours – I thought you could use the mood machine to come out of them. But when you're very depressed, you don't care. You have no worth . . .'

'What about your job?' Iran said sharply. 'Your job,' she repeated. 'I'm glad you got the goat, but now we've got all those monthly payments. Don't forget that.'

The videophone rang. Rick froze.

'I'm not here,' he said, and went into the bedroom.

'Hello,' Iran greeted the caller. 'Yes, he's here. We bought a goat. Come and see it, Mr Bryant.' There was a pause while she listened and then she called to Rick. 'He has something to say to you.'

Iran left the phone and went to the empathy box. Rick was suddenly very conscious of being alone.

'We have some information about two of the other androids,' Bryant told him. 'They've left the address that Dave gave you, and they've gone to . . . yes, Conapt Building 3967-C. Leave as soon as you can. They probably know about the ones you killed; that's the reason for their unlawful flight.'

'Unlawful,' Rick repeated. To save their lives.

'I'll come and look at your goat after you've killed them,' Bryant said. 'Oh, and I spoke to Dave. He says congratulations and be careful. These Nexus-6 types are more intelligent than we imagine.'

'OK,' Rick said slowly, 'I'll go now. If I get them, I'm going to buy a sheep.'

'You have a sheep. You've had it all the time I've known you.'

'It's electric,' Rick said. He hung up. A real sheep this time, he thought. I have to get one. A life for a death.

His wife stood at the black empathy box, her face lit with deep happiness. He stood beside her with his hand on her chest, feeling it rise and fall; the life in her, the activity. Iran did not notice him. She was with Mercer.

Rick watched the picture of Mercer climbing upwards, rocks flying past him. My god, Rick thought, there's something worse about my situation than his. He feels pain, but at least he can be true to himself. Rick took his wife's hands gently from the handles and put his own there for the first time in weeks.

He was in a desert, and a man stood in front of him.

'Mercer,' Rick said.

'I am your friend,' the man said, 'but you must continue without me. Can you understand that?'

'No,' Rick said. 'I need help.'

69

'How can I save you if I can't save myself?' The old man smiled.

'Then what's this for?' Rick demanded. 'What are *you* for?'

'To show you,' Wilbur Mercer said, 'that you aren't alone. I am here with you and I always will be. Do your job even if you know it's wrong.'

'Why?' asked Rick. 'Why should I? I'll leave my job and emigrate.'

The old man said, 'You will not be asked to do wrong. Every creature which lives sometimes has to do things it doesn't believe in. We all have to accept that.'

A flying rock hit Rick on the ear, and he took his hands off the handles. His head hurt and blood was running down his face. Iran cleaned it for him.

'I guess I'm glad you took me off the box,' she said. 'Thank you for taking the rock in my place.'

'I'm going,' Rick said.

'The job?'

'Three jobs.' He went to the door. He was feeling sick now.

'Good luck!' Iran said.

'I didn't get anything from holding those handles,' Rick told her. 'Mercer doesn't know any more than I do. He's just an old man climbing a hill to his death.'

'Isn't that what we have to learn?'

'I already knew that. I'll see you later.'

Conapt 3967-C, Rick thought. That's in the suburbs. A good place to hide, except for the lights at night. I'll look for the lights. And then, after this, I'll earn my salary doing something else. These three are my last. But, he worried, can

I actually kill three? I'm tired, sick and alone . . . But I know where I can find help.

He reached the roof and sat in his hovercar, dialling.

'Rachael Rosen, please,' he said.

A few minutes later, Rachael's face appeared. 'Hello, Mr Deckard. Your ear is cut.'

'Did you think I wouldn't call you?'

'Well, you're calling now. Do you want me to come to San Francisco?'

'Tonight.'

'Oh, it's too late. I'll come tomorrow.'

'I have to get them tonight.' He paused. 'There are only three out of the eight left. If you don't come, I'll have to try alone and I won't manage it. I just bought a goat,' he added, 'with the money from the three I got earlier.'

'You humans,' Rachael laughed. 'Goats smell terrible.'

'Only male goats.'

'You look really tired,' Rachael said. 'Are you sure you're ready for more? Nobody has ever killed six androids in one day. Look, Rick, I can't come until tomorrow.'

'Fly down here now and we'll rent a hotel room,' Rick suggested.

'Why?'

'Something I heard about human men and android women. If you share a room with me, I won't go after the other androids today.'

She looked at him carefully. 'OK,' she said suddenly, 'I'll meet you at the St Francis Hotel. But you won't do anything until I arrive?'

'I'll sit in the room and watch Buster Friendly on television,'

71

he said and hung up. He thought for a while until he began to feel the cold. Then he started the hovercar and flew in the direction of the St Francis Hotel.

Later, in the large, expensive hotel room, Rick sat reading the typed sheets of information about Roy and Irmgard Baty. There were photographs. The woman, he decided, looked pretty. Roy Baty, though, was different. Worse. Baty had run a shop on Mars, he read. Or that's what the android *said*. He had probably just worked in the fields or with his hands. Do androids dream? Rick asked himself. Probably. That was why they killed their employers and escaped to Earth, looking for a better life as free individuals. Like Luba Luft, singing Mozart at the opera house.

The report on Roy Baty described him as a rough, cold android. He had killed a number of people before he left and probably still took mind-changing drugs. He was the father figure of a group that hoped, through the use of such drugs, to provide for androids an experience similar to Mercerism.

The door burst open.

'What a flight!' Rachael Rosen cried. 'Less than an hour. This is a nice room. Here . . .' She passed Rick a bag. 'I brought some whisky.'

'The worst of the eight is still alive,' Rick said. 'Roy Baty.'

'Do you know where he is?' Rachael asked.

'Yes, he's out in the suburbs.'

'And the others?'

'Both females.' He gave her the sheets. She looked at them and then went to the window. She said nothing.

'What's the matter?' Rick asked her, watching her back.

'Tell me what we're going to do instead of worrying about

those androids,' she ordered, turning to face him. She took her coat off and he was able to examine her properly for the first time. Rachael had, he noticed, the body of a child, and her thick, dark hair made her head seem larger than it should be. Only her big eyes were the eyes of a woman.

Rachael sat down next to him on the bed, and they drank some whisky.

'What upset you?' Rick asked again.

'That last Nexus-6 female, Pris Stratton, is the same type as I am. Didn't you notice the description? She may wear her hair differently and dress in different clothes, but you'll know what I mean when you see her. And I'll be there when you kill her. I think you're asking too much.' She lay down on the bed and shut her eyes. 'Let's forget them. I'm tired.' Her eyes suddenly opened again. 'Do you know why I'm really here... why Eldon Rosen sent me?'

'To watch the Voigt-Kampff test,' Rick said, 'and see how it traps the Nexus-6.'

'Yes, to notice anything that will help us build the Nexus-7. And when you can catch that, we'll change the design again. In the end there'll be an android that you can't find. Now take off your coat.'

'Why?'

'So we can go to bed.'

He realized how frightened he was of his final challenge; of Baty, the leader.

'I can't go without you now,' he told Rachael. He was walking round the room. 'I can't even leave here. Polokov came after me; Garland more or less came after me.'

'You think Roy Baty is looking for you too? Come here.'

The drink had obviously had an effect, because she was smiling at him. He walked slowly to the bed and undressed her.

'How does it feel to be born?' she asked. 'We're not born and we don't grow up.' She rolled on to her side and laughed. 'I'm not alive! You're not going to bed with a woman. Don't be disappointed, OK? Have you ever made love to an android before?'

'No,' he said, taking off his shirt and tie.

'They tell me it's almost the same if you don't think too much about it. And if you do think about it, you can't continue.'

He kissed her shoulder.

'I love you,' Rachael told him. 'If I entered a room and found a sofa covered in your skin, I'd score very high on the Voigt-Kampff test.'

Some time tonight, he thought as he turned off the bedside light, I will kill a Nexus-6 which looks just like this girl. Good god, he thought; I'm taking Phil Resch's advice. Go to bed with her first, he remembered. Then kill her.

'I can't do it,' he said and moved off the bed.

'I wish you could,' Rachael said. Her voice was warm.

'Not because of you. Because of Pris Stratton; what I have to do to her.'

'We're not the same. I don't care about Pris Stratton. Listen . . . Come to bed with me and *I'll* kill Stratton.'

'Thank you,' he said gratefully. Would Rachael really do it? It seemed that an android could in fact kill another android.

'Now get into bed!' Rachael ordered.

He got into bed.

Afterwards they enjoyed the luxury of coffee brought up by room service. Then Rachael sat in the bath and sang.

'You made a good deal with me,' she called. 'You knew that we androids can't control our feelings. You took advantage of me.' She seemed as human as any woman that Rick had ever known. 'Do we really have to kill those androids tonight?'

'Yes,' he answered. Two for me, he thought, and one for you.

Rachael came out of the bathroom wrapped in a large white towel.

'I've been in existence for two years now,' she said. 'How much longer do you think I've got?'

He hesitated. 'About two more years. I'm sorry.'

She dried herself. 'No – I'm sorry I said anything. Anyway, it stops humans running off and living with androids.'

They dressed and travelled together up to the roof field. Then they headed towards the suburbs of San Francisco.

'My goat is probably asleep by now,' Rick said. 'Or maybe it doesn't sleep at night. I don't know.'

'What kind of wife do you have?'

Rick did not answer.

'Do you . . .?' She hesitated.

'If you weren't an android,' Rick told her, 'if I could marry you by law, I would.'

'You look so sad.'

He stretched out his hand and touched her face.

'You're not going to be able to kill androids any more,' she went on calmly. 'So don't look sad. Please.'

He stared at her.

'No android killer has ever gone on after being with me,'

Rachael said. 'Except one. Phil Resch. And he's crazy.'

'I see,' said Rick. His whole body was frozen in his seat. He had no feeling in any part of it.

'But now you're going to meet a wonderful man,' Rachael continued.

'Roy Baty,' he said. 'Do you know all of them?'

'I knew all of them, when they still existed. I know three now. We tried to stop you this morning when I rang you, but then we had to wait.'

'Until I broke down and called *you*.'

'Luba Luft and I were very good friends. What did you think of her? Did you like her?'

'I liked her.'

'But you killed her.'

'Phil Resch killed her.'

'Ah, we didn't know that. Only that she had been killed. We thought by you.'

'So everything that happened at the hotel was just a . . . How many times have you done this?' Rick asked.

'I don't remember. Seven or eight times. Nine. It's a useful weapon.'

'The idea is very old-fashioned,' Rick said and started landing the hovercar. 'I'm going to kill you now. And then I'll go on alone and kill the others.'

'You can't do that,' she said nervously. 'I belong to the corporation. I didn't escape from Mars.'

'But,' he reminded her, 'if I can kill you, I can kill them.'

The life force was leaving her. He had seen it before with androids. Calm, mechanical acceptance, where a human, desperate to survive, would fight on to the end.

'Will you do it carefully?' she asked quietly. 'So that it doesn't hurt?'

He landed the car and took out his laser gun.

'At the bottom of my head,' Rachael said, turning away from him and pointing to the back of her neck. 'Here. Please.'

He stared at her, then he put the gun away and a moment later they took off again. He flew back towards the St Francis Hotel, where she had left her car.

'Thank you for not killing me,' Rachael said.

'Thank you for not killing me.'

'Well, you've only got two years and I've got fifty,' Rick replied.

'You're the same as the others.' Rachael sounded more confident now. 'You all get angry and talk about killing me. I'm right, you know. You won't be able to kill the others. So go home to your goat. You love that goat more than me. More than you love your wife, probably.' She laughed.

He did not answer. They continued in silence for a while and then Rachael found the car radio and turned it on.

'No,' Rick said.

'Don't you want to listen to Buster Friendly and his friendly friends? It's almost time for his great piece of news. Did you know about that? He's been talking about it for . . .'

Rick turned the radio off. Rachael turned it on again. 'I want to listen. This is important, what Buster Friendly has to say on his show tonight.'

She sat back in her seat as Buster's voice flooded the speakers once again. She had beaten him.

8

Surprises

'Bring the rest of my things up here,' Pris ordered J.R. Isidore. 'I want my television so we can hear Buster's news.'

'Yes,' Irmgard agreed, bright-eyed. 'We need the television; we've been waiting a long time for tonight and it'll be starting soon.'

Alone, Isidore walked down the dark, empty hall to the stairs. He was still bursting with happiness, with a sense of being useful for the first time in his dull life. Others depend on me now, he thought as he stepped through the dirt on the stairs to the floor below. And it'll be nice to see Buster Friendly on television again, instead of just listening to him on the truck radio. It is tonight, he realized, that Buster has promised to surprise us. So because of Pris and Roy and Irmgard I shall watch what is probably the most important news broadcast for years.

Life, for J.R. Isidore, had certainly got better.

He entered the apartment that Pris had been living in and picked up the television. The silence was starting to worry him, and his arms felt weak. You have to be with people, he thought. Before they came here, I could stand it, being alone in the building. But now it's changed. I need them. Thank god they stayed.

He decided to carry the television up first and then return for the bags and clothes. When he reached his own living room, he put the television down on a table.

'The picture's good in this building,' he said, breathing hard. 'When I used to get Buster . . .'

'Just turn it on and stop talking,' Roy said.

He did so, then hurried to the door.

'One more trip,' he told them.

'Fine,' Pris answered, her eyes on the television.

I think, Isidore thought as he went downstairs again, they're using me. But he didn't care. They're good friends to have, he said to himself.

On a step below him, something moved in the dust. He stopped immediately and took out a plastic medicine bottle which, like everyone else, he carried with him at all times for this purpose. A spider, and it was alive. He carefully guided it into the bottle and put the lid on. There were tiny breathing holes in the top. He ran back upstairs.

' . . . yes, sir; the time is *now*. This is Buster Friendly, who hopes you're all ready to share the discovery which I've made and which top investigators have checked for me. Ho, ho, this is it!'

John Isidore said, 'I found a spider.'

The three androids gave him a quick look, turning their attention from the television for a moment.

'Let's see it,' Pris said. She held out her hand.

'Don't talk while Buster's on,' said Roy Baty.

'I've never seen a spider,' Pris said, the bottle cupped in her hand. 'All those legs. Why does it need so many legs, J.R?'

'That's the way spiders are,' Isidore replied. 'Eight legs.'

Standing up, Pris said, 'Do you know what I think, J.R? I think it doesn't need all those legs.'

'Eight?' said Irmgard. 'Maybe four are enough. Cut four off and see.' She took a pair of scissors out of her bag and passed them to Pris.

J.R. Isidore experienced a strange sense of terror.

Carrying the medicine bottle into the kitchen, Pris sat down, took the lid off the bottle, and knocked the spider out onto Isidore's breakfast table. 'It probably won't be able to run as fast,' she said, 'but there's nothing for it to eat around here. It'll die anyway.' She reached for the scissors.

'Please,' Isidore said.

Pris looked up at him. 'Is it worth something?'

'Don't hurt it,' he begged.

With the scissors, Pris cut off one of the spider's legs. In the living room, Buster Friendly said, 'Look at this picture. This is the sky that you normally see on the screens of your empathy boxes. Now Earl Parameter, one of my investigators, will explain our world-shaking discovery to you.' Pris cut off another leg, holding the spider with the edge of her hand. She was smiling.

'When the video pictures are made larger,' the investigator continued, 'we can see that the grey sky against which Mercer moves is not real.'

'You're missing it,' Irmgard called anxiously to Pris. She rushed to the kitchen door to see what Pris was doing. 'Oh, do that afterwards,' she said, 'this is so important. It proves that everything we believed . . .'

'Be quiet,' Roy Baty said.

' . . . is true,' Irmgard finished.

The television broadcast continued. 'We can see here that the moon is obviously painted, and the dry ground is false. It is quite possible that the stones are made of soft plastic and do not in fact hurt.'

'In other words,' Buster Friendly said, 'Wilbur Mercer is not in pain at all.'

'We managed, Mr Friendly,' the investigator told him, 'using thousands of photographs, to find a very old man called Al Jarry, who used to act in films before the war. We went to his home in East Harmony, Virginia, and he told us that he did once make a number of short fifteen-minute video films for an employer that he never met. The rocks they threw at him were in fact plastic, the blood was paint, and the only pain that Mr Jarry experienced was a whole day without whisky.' The investigator laughed.

'Al Jarry,' Buster Friendly said as his face reappeared. 'Al Jarry made a few dull films and did not know who they were for. People have said that Wilbur Mercer is not a human being, that he is something much greater, perhaps from another planet. Well, in a sense they are correct. Wilbur Mercer is not human, does not in fact exist. The world in which he climbs is a cheap, Hollywood setting which disappeared into the dust years ago. And who, then, started this joke?'

'We may never know,' Irmgard whispered.

'We may never know,' Buster continued. 'But we *do* know that Mercerism is nothing more than an invention. Yes, Mercer is a fake.'

'I think we know,' Roy Baty said. 'Mercerism came into existence . . .'

'But think about this.' Buster Friendly was still talking.

'Ask yourself what Mercerism does. Well, if we're to believe those who practise it, Mercerism brings men and women on every planet together. And how is this done? By the so-called voice of 'Mercer', a . . .'

'No,' said Irmgard angrily, walking up to Isidore, 'it's a way of proving that humans can do something we can't, isn't it? Because without your Mercerism, we only have your word that you feel this empathy, this shared group thing. How's the spider?' She bent over Pris' shoulder.

'Four gone,' Pris replied. She pushed the spider. 'He won't move. But he can.'

Roy Baty appeared in the doorway. 'It's done. Buster said it and almost every human heard him. Mercerism is meaningless.' He looked curiously at the spider.

'It won't walk,' Irmgard told him.

'I can make it walk.' Roy took out some matches and lit one; he held it near the spider until at last it moved slowly away.

'I was right,' Irmgard said. 'It can walk on four legs.' She looked up at Isidore. 'What's the matter? You won't lose anything. We'll pay you what . . . that Sydney's guide says it's worth. Don't look so unhappy. Isn't that interesting, what they discovered about Mercer? Hey, answer me.' She pushed him anxiously.

'He's upset,' Pris said, 'because he has an empathy box in the other room. Do you use it, J.R?'

'Of course he uses it. They all do – or did. Maybe now they'll start wondering.' Roy smiled.

'This won't end it,' Pris said. 'But now there are a lot of unhappy human beings.' To Isidore she said: 'We've waited for months. We knew this was coming.' She hesitated, then said, 'Well, why not. Buster is one of us.'

'An android,' Irmgard explained. 'And nobody knows. No humans, I mean.'

Pris, with the scissors, cut another leg off the spider. Suddenly John Isidore pushed her away and lifted the creature from the table. He carried it to the tap, turned the water on, and drowned it. His mind, his hopes, drowned too. As quickly as the spider.

'He's really upset,' Irmgard said nervously. 'Don't look like that, J.R. And why don't you say anything?' To Pris and her husband, she said, 'He hasn't spoken since we turned the television on.'

'It's not the television, it's the spider – isn't it, John R. Isidore? He'll be all right,' Pris said to Irmgard, who had gone into the other room to turn the television off.

Looking at Isidore with amusement, Roy Baty said, 'It's all finished now. Mercerism, I mean.' He picked up the dead spider. 'Maybe this was the last spider,' he added thoughtfully. 'The last living spider on Earth. In that case it's finished for spiders too.'

'I . . . don't feel well,' Isidore said. He took a cup out of a kitchen cupboard and stood holding it for a while – he didn't know for how long. 'Is the sky behind Mercer really just painted?' he suddenly asked Roy.

'You saw the lines from the paintbrush on the television.'

'Mercerism isn't finished,' Isidore said. There was something wrong with these androids, very wrong. The spider, he thought. Maybe it was the last spider on earth, as Roy Baty said. And the spider is gone; Mercer is gone. He saw the dust spreading and the rubbish covering the empty buildings, the end of everything. He heard the cupboards in his kitchen breaking and falling, and he felt the ground under his feet begin to move.

He touched the wall, and his hand went through it. He sat down, and the legs of the chair bent. The cup in his hand was in little pieces.

'What's he doing?' Irmgard's voice came to him. 'He's breaking everything. Isidore, stop!'

'I'm not doing it,' he said. He walked slowly into the living room, to be alone, and looked around. It's all old, he thought, and it's being destroyed. He saw pieces of animals, grey bones, and as he walked he felt them breaking under his shoes. It's happening to me again, he realized. I'll be down here a long time. Like before.

The wind blew, and more bones broke. I wish I could remember how to climb up from here, he thought. Looking up, he could see nothing to hold on to. Mercer, he said, where are you now? I'm down here, but this time you're not here with me.

Something crossed his foot. He bent down and looked for it – and found it because it moved so slowly. The spider, walking on its remaining legs; he picked it up and held it in his hands. The spider is alive, he realized. Mercer must be near.

The wind blew again and broke the bones, but he felt the presence of Mercer. Come here, he said to Mercer. 'Mercer!' Suddenly the face of the old man was in front of him, a calm expression on his face.

'Is the sky painted?' Isidore asked. 'Are there really lines from the brush?'

'Yes,' Mercer said.

'I can't see them.'

'You are too near,' Mercer answered. 'You have to be a long way away, like the androids. They see things more clearly. It's all true, you know, what they said.'

'Including about the whisky?'

'It was all true. They will have trouble understanding why nothing's changed. Because you're still here and I'm still here. I lifted you from the bones just now, and I will continue to lift you until you want to stop. But you will have to stop searching for me, because I will never stop searching for you.'

'I didn't like that, about the whisky.'

'That's because you are a very good person. I'm not. I don't judge — not even myself.' Mercer held out his hand. 'Before I forget, I have something that belongs to you.' On his hand rested the spider, but with all its eight legs.

'Thank you.' Isidore accepted the spider. He started to say something else, but then the alarm rang.

'There's a killer in the building!' Roy Baty shouted. 'Turn the lights off. Get Isidore away from that empathy box; he has to be ready at the door. Move him!'

Looking down, Isidore saw his hands on the handles of the empathy box. The lights went out, and he heard Irmgard's voice in his ear.

'Listen, J.R.,' she whispered. Anger and fear suddenly made her look ugly. 'You have to go to the door, when he knocks — if he knocks. You must show him your identification and tell him this is your apartment and nobody else is here.'

Pris, on the other side of him now, whispered in his other ear. 'Don't let him in, J.R. Say anything; do anything to stop him. Do you understand what he would do to us if he found us?'

Moving away from them, Isidore made his way through the dark to the door. He stood there and listened. He could sense the hall outside, as he always sensed it: empty and lifeless.

'Can you hear anything?' Roy Baty bent near him, and Isidore could smell his fear. 'Step outside and have a look.'

Isidore opened the door. He was still holding the spider which Mercer had given him. Was it the same spider that Pris had cut with her scissors? Probably not. He would never know. But at least it was alive. He walked to the end of the hall and down the stairs, and stepped into the garden. Most of the plants had died, and the broken paths were covered with dust, but it felt good to feel the familiar ground under his feet. He found a small area of half-dead grass and put the spider carefully down on it. Then he stood up again.

9

Last battles

The light of a torch shone on the grass. Now Isidore could see the spider resting on a leaf. So it was all right now.

'What did you do?' asked the man holding the torch.

'I put down a spider,' Isidore answered, wondering why the man did not see it. 'So it could escape.'

'Why don't you take it up to your apartment and put it in a bottle? The price in Sydney's for a spider is a hundred and ten dollars.'

'If I took it back there, she'd cut its legs off again. One by one, to see what it would do.'

'Androids do that,' the man said. He took a card from his pocket and showed it to Isidore. 'I work for the San Francisco Police. Deckard. Rick Deckard.' He put the card away again. 'They're up there now? The three of them?'

'Actually,' Isidore said, 'I'm looking after them. Two are women. They're the last ones of the group; the others are dead. I brought Pris's television up from her apartment and put it in mine, so that they could watch Buster Friendly. Buster proved that Mercer doesn't exist.' Isidore was excited that he knew something important – news that the killer obviously hadn't heard.

'Let's go up there,' Deckard said. He pointed his laser gun

at Isidore; then, a moment later, he put it away again. 'You're a special, aren't you?' he said. 'A chickenhead.'

'But I have a job. I drive a truck for . . .' He hesitated, forgetting the name. ' . . . for a pet hospital. The Van Ness Pet Hospital. Owned b-b-by Hannibal Sloat.'

Deckard said, 'Will you take me up there and show me which apartment they're in? You can save me a lot of time – there are more than a thousand apartments.' He sounded exhausted.

'If you kill them, you won't be able to become one with Mercer again,' Isidore told him.

'You won't take me up? Tell me which floor?'

'No,' said Isidore.

'By law, . . .' Deckard began. Then he stopped. 'Good night,' he said, and walked away towards the building, following the path with his torchlight.

Inside the building, Rick turned off his torch and made his way slowly along the hall. The chickenhead knew they were androids before I told him, he thought. But he doesn't understand. On the other hand, who does? Do I? Did I? And one of them will look exactly like Rachael, he reminded himself. Maybe the special has been living with her. I wonder how he liked it.

He had brought his listening equipment from the car. In the silence of the hall, it showed no sounds. Not on this floor. He changed the controls to a vertical reading. Upstairs, he noted. He climbed the stairs to the next floor.

A figure was waiting in the shadows.

'If you move, I'll kill you,' Rick said. The male one. The laser gun felt heavy in his hand. He tried to lift it but couldn't.

'I'm not an android,' the figure said. 'My name is Mercer. I inhabit this building because of Mr Isidore. The special who had the spider – you spoke to him outside.'

'Am I outside Mercerism now?' Rick asked. 'As the chickenhead said? Because of what I'm going to do in the next few minutes?'

Mercer answered, 'Mr Isidore spoke for himself, not for me. What you are doing has to be done.' He pointed at the stairs behind Rick. 'I came to tell you that one of them is behind you and below, not in the apartment. It will be the hard one of the three, and you must kill it first. Quick, Mr Deckard. On the steps.'

Rick turned and dropped to his knees. There was a woman, and he knew her. He lowered his laser gun.

'Rachael,' he said. Had she followed him in her own hovercar? Why? 'Go back to Seattle,' he told her. 'Leave me alone.' And then he saw that it was not Rachael.

'Come here, my dear,' the android said, holding out its arms. The clothes, he thought, are wrong. But the eyes, the same eyes. And there are more like this, each with its own name, but all Rachael Rosens. He fired at her as her eyes begged him not to. The android burst and parts of it flew towards him; he covered his face. The hard one of the three, Mercer had said. He looked in the shadows, searching for Mercer, but the old man had gone. They can follow me with Rachael Rosens until I die, he thought, or until they invent a Nexus-7 type.

And now the other two. Mercer protected me, he realized. Offered help. And now I can do the rest. The Batys will be hard, but they won't be like this. Somewhere in the building the Batys waited and knew. Probably, at this point, they were afraid. Rachael – or Pris Stratton – was their best weapon, and without Mercer it would have worked.

He took out his equipment again and hurried down the hall. Here. He had found the apartment. He knocked on the door.

A man's voice answered. 'Who is it?'

'This is Mr Isidore,' Rick said. 'Let me in because I'm looking after you and t-t-two of you are women.'

'We're not opening the door,' said a woman's voice.

'I want to watch Buster Friendly on Pris's television,' Rick called. 'I d-drive a truck for the Van Ness Pet Hospital,' he added. 'Would you p-p-please open the d-d-door.'

He waited and the door opened. There were two shapes in the dark apartment.

The smaller shape, the woman, said, 'You have to do the tests.'

'It's too late,' Rick told her. The taller figure tried to shut the door and turn on some electrical equipment. 'No,' Rick said. 'I have to come in.' He moved quickly to one side as Roy Baty fired at him. 'You shouldn't have done that,' Rick shouted. 'I can now kill you without the test.' Roy Baty fired again, missed, and ran into another room.

'Why didn't Pris get you?' Mrs Baty asked.

'There is no Pris,' he told her. 'Only hundreds of Rachael Rosens.' He saw the gun in her hand; her husband must have passed it to her as he ran to the back. 'I'm sorry, Mrs Baty,' Rick said, and shot her.

Roy Baty, in the shadows, screamed.

'OK, you loved her,' Rick said. 'And I loved Rachael. And

the special loved the other Rachael.' He shot Roy Baty. The big man's body fell onto the kitchen table. Plates and glasses flew in all directions. Then the body hit the ground. I got the last one, Rick thought. Six today. And now it's finished and I can go back home to Iran and the goat. And we'll finally have enough money.

'It's too late.'

He sat down on the sofa. After a few minutes the special, Mr Isidore, appeared in the doorway.

'Don't look,' Rick said.

'I saw her on the stairs. Pris.' The special was crying.

'Don't get upset,' Rick said. He stood up slowly. 'Where's your phone?'

The special said nothing, so Rick searched for it himself. When he found it, he dialled Harry Bryant's office.

'Good,' Bryant said, after he had been told the news. 'Well, go and get some rest. We'll send a car for the bodies.'

Rick hung up. 'Androids are stupid,' he told the special angrily. 'Roy Baty thought I was you. The police will clean all this. Why don't you stay in another apartment until they've finished?'

'I'm leaving this b-b-building,' Isidore said. 'I'm g-g-going to live nearer the centre where there are m-m-more people.'

'I think there's an empty apartment in my building,' Rick said.

'I don't w-w-want to live near you!'

'Go outside or upstairs,' Rick said. 'Don't stay in here.'

The special hesitated. A number of different expressions crossed his face and then, turning, he left the apartment. Rick was alone again.

What a job! Rick thought. As Mercer says, it's my job to do wrong. Everything I've done has been wrong, from start to finish. But now it's time to go home. Perhaps there I can forget.

10

Journey's end

Iran met Rick on the roof of their apartment building. She looked at him in a strange, crazy way; in all his years with her, he had never seen her like this. He put his arms around her.

'It's finished now,' he said quietly. 'I've been thinking that maybe Bryant can find me another job . . .'

'Rick,' his wife said. 'I have to tell you something. I'm sorry. The goat's dead.'

For some reason it did not surprise him; it only made him feel worse. 'I think there's something in the agreement,' he said. 'If it gets sick within ninety days, the dealer . . .'

'It didn't get sick. Someone . . .' Iran stopped and covered her eyes for a moment. 'Someone came here and pushed it off the roof.'

'Did you see who did it?'

'I saw her very clearly,' Iran said. 'Barbour was still up here with his horse. He came to find me and we called the police, but when they arrived it was too late. The animal was dead and she'd left. A small young-looking girl with dark hair and large black eyes, very thin. She didn't try to hide – she didn't seem to care if we saw her.'

'No, she didn't care,' Rick agreed. 'Rachael probably wanted you to see her, so I'd know who did it.' He kissed her. 'Have you been waiting here all this time?'

'Only for half an hour. That's when it happened – half an hour ago.' Iran gently returned the kiss. 'It's so awful. So meaningless.'

Rick opened his car door and got in behind the wheel. 'She had what seemed to her a reason,' he said. An android reason, he thought.

'Where are you going? Won't you come downstairs and ... be with me? There was shocking news on television; Buster Friendly said that Mercer was a fake. What do you think, Rick? Could it be true?'

'Everything is true,' he replied. 'Everything that anybody has thought.' He started the car.

'Will you be all right?'

'I'll be all right,' he said. I'm going to die, he thought. That's true too. He waved to Iran and drove up into the sky.

Once, Rick thought, you could see the stars. But now it's only dust. Nobody has seen a star for years – at least not from Earth. Maybe I'll go to a place where I can see stars, he said to himself. He turned the car away from San Francisco towards the uninhabited areas to the north. Towards a place where no living thing ever went, unless it felt that the end had come.

In the early morning light, the land below him seemed to continue for ever, grey and covered in stones and rubbish. Once, he reminded himself, plants grew and animals lived here. I'm exhausted, he thought; I shouldn't be flying. He landed the hovercar at the bottom of a rocky hill.

What would Dave Holden say about me now? Six androids in twenty-four hours. I ought to call him. He picked up the car phone and dialled. 'Mount Zion Hospital?' he checked. 'You have a patient called Dave Holden. Is he well enough for me to talk to him? It's police business.'

'Just a moment, sir . . . No, sir. Dr Costa does not feel that Mr Holden should take any calls for at least . . .'

'OK,' Rick said, and hung up. Dave's condition is really serious, he thought. I wonder why Bryant didn't tell me. Because I was moving too fast, he decided. Bryant was right not to let me know.

It was cold in the car now, so Rick opened the door and stepped out. He was hit by a terrible-smelling wind, and he rubbed his hands, trying to keep warm. Dave would have understood, he knew . . . even the other part, which I don't think even Mercer understands. For Mercer everything is easy, because he accepts everything. But what I've done *I* can't accept. I've become unnatural to myself.

He walked on up the hillside, more slowly with every step. Too tired, he thought, to climb. He stopped for a moment. His whole body ached. He was angry, hating himself. Then, alone on the hill, he began to climb again.

It was hot now. Obviously time had passed. And he was hungry; god knows how long it was since he last ate. Defeat, that was what he felt. I've been defeated in some way. By killing the androids? By Rachael's murder of my goat? He did not know. Suddenly he fell on the stones, and at that moment the first rock – and it was not a plastic rock – hit him. The pain was greater than he had ever experienced.

'Mercer!' he cried. In front of him, he could see a figure. 'Wilbur Mercer! Is that you?' My god, he realized, it's my own shadow. I have to get away, down off this hill. He ran back down again. Once he fell, and clouds of dust rose from the ground. He hurried on until he saw his car, then jumped inside. Who threw the rock at me? he wondered. Nobody. But why does it worry me? I've experienced all this before, using the empathy box. Because, he realized, this time I was alone.

He looked at his watch. Nine-thirty. He dialled the police station. 'Give me Inspector Bryant,' he said.

'Inspector Bryant is not in his office, Mr Deckard,' an officer answered.

'Let me speak to his secretary, then.'

The secretary's face appeared on the screen. 'Oh, Mr Deckard, Inspector Bryant has been trying to find you. Congratulations on killing all those androids. Oh, and Mr Deckard, your wife phoned. She wants to know if you're all right. Are you?'

He said nothing.

'Maybe you should call her. She's at home, waiting to hear from you. Mr Deckard, you look awful. So tired. And you're bleeding.'

He lifted his hand and felt the blood.

'You look,' the secretary went on, 'like Wilbur Mercer.'

'I am,' he said. 'I'm Wilbur Mercer; I've become one with him, and I've lost myself. I'm somewhere up in the state of Oregon.'

'Come back to San Francisco, Mr Deckard, where there are people. Aren't you all alone up there?'

'I'm alone,' he agreed, 'but I've become Mercer. Not the way you experience it when you hold the handles of an empathy box. Then you're *with* Mercer. I'm not with anyone.'

'They're saying now that Mercer's a fake.'

'Mercer isn't a fake,' he told her, 'unless reality is a fake.' I'm afraid, he thought, that I can't stop being Mercer. Will I have to climb that hill for ever? 'Good-bye,' he said.

I need bed rest, he told himself. The last time I was in bed was with Rachael Rosen. Sleeping with an android – against the law, here and on the other planets. She must be in Seattle now with the other Rosens, humans and androids. If I had killed her last night, my goat would still be alive. That's when I made a wrong decision. Well, she was correct about one

But they're all dead.

98

thing; the experience did change me. But not in the way that she expected. A much worse way, he decided.

But I don't really care now. Not after what happened to me up there on the hill. If I'm Mercer, he thought, I can never die, not in ten thousand years. He picked up the phone to call his wife. And froze.

He put the phone down again and stared at the place where something had moved. An animal, he said to himself. I know what it is, he realized, from the old nature films they show on television. But they're all dead. He quickly pulled out his Sydney's guide and turned the pages to **TOAD**. There were no toads in existence.

A box. He looked in the back of the car and found one full of tools. He emptied it quickly and walked towards the toad. It was yellowish-brown, the same colour as the dust. If it hadn't moved, he wouldn't have noticed it. What happens if

you find the only animal of its kind? He tried to remember. You got some kind of prize from the United Nations, and a lot of money, he thought. This can't be true. Perhaps it's the effect of the radioactive dust. I'm a special now. It's like Isidore finding the spider. Did Mercer arrange this? But *I'm* Mercer. I arranged it. I found the toad because I see through Mercer's eyes.

He carefully brushed the dirt off the toad and lifted it into the box. He shut the box and carried it to the car. This is what Mercer sees, he thought; life in the dust. And now that I've seen through Mercer's eyes once, I probably won't stop. Wait until Iran hears about this. He got back into the car, put the box on the passenger seat, and started to dial. Then paused. It'll be a surprise for her, he decided. He set out for San Francisco, seven hundred miles to the south.

Back in the apartment, Iran was sitting beside her mood machine. But she felt too miserable and ill to dial a new mood. If Rick were here, she thought, he'd dial for me. I wonder where he is . . . and if he'll come back.

There was a knock at the door.

Rick! She jumped up and opened the door wide.

'Hello!' he said. There was blood on his face and dust in his clothes, but his eyes shone like the eyes of a small boy.

'It's nice to see you,' she said.

'I have something.' He held a box, but did not put it down as he came in. It's something so valuable to him, she thought, that he wants to keep it in his arms.

She said, 'I'll make you a cup of coffee.'

While she made it, he sat down, and the bright expression remained on his face. Something had happened since she last saw him, and he held in that box everything that had happened.

'I'm going to sleep,' he told her. 'All day. I need to rest.' He put the box on the table and, because she wanted him to, drank his coffee.

'What do you have in the box, Rick?'

'A toad.'

'Can I see it?'

He opened the box. For some reason she felt afraid.

'Will it bite?' She picked it up gently.

'No, toads don't have teeth. I found it in Oregon, in the desert where everything else had died.' He reached to take it back, but she had discovered something. She showed him the tiny control box near the toad's stomach.

'Oh. Yes, I see,' he said sadly. He looked at the false animal without quite understanding. 'I wonder how it got to Oregon. Somebody must have put it there.'

'Perhaps I shouldn't have showed you.' She touched his arm.

'No,' Rick said. 'I'm glad to know. Or . . . I'd prefer to know.'

'Do you want to use the mood machine?' Iran asked. 'To feel better?'

'I'll be OK.' He shook his head. 'The spider that Mercer gave the chickenhead, Isidore; it was probably false too. But it doesn't matter. These electrical things have lives too, although they're poorer than ours.'

'Go and sleep,' Iran told him.

He looked at her, still confused. 'It's finished, isn't it?'

'It's finished.'

'What a job,' Rick said. 'After I'd started, I couldn't stop. Then after I'd finished, I couldn't stop because there would be nothing left if I did stop. You were right this morning when you said I was worse than a policeman.'

'I don't feel that now,' she said. 'I'm just so happy to have you back here where you belong.' She kissed him and that seemed to please him. His eyes shone again, in the way they did before she found the controls for the toad.

'You must have heard all about it from Bryant,' he said. 'Do you think I did wrong? What I did today?'

'No.'

'Mercer said it was wrong but I should do it anyway. Sometimes it's better to do something wrong than right.'

'When the killers found Mercer in his sixteenth year,' Iran said, 'they told him that he couldn't bring things to life again. So now he can only move along with life, going where it goes, to death. And the killers throw the rocks; they're still chasing him. And all of us. Did one of them cut your face, where it's bleeding?'

'Yes,' he said weakly.

'Will you go to bed now if I dial 670 on your mood machine for you?'

'What does that bring?'

'Peace.'

He stood up painfully and walked slowly to the bedroom. 'OK,' he agreed, 'peace.' He lay on the bed, and dust fell on to the sheets from his hair and clothes.

She didn't need to turn on the mood machine, Iran realized. On the bed Rick, after a moment, slept.

She stayed with him for a while and then returned to the

kitchen and sat down. Next to her on the table, the electric toad was moving in its box. What did it eat? False flies, she decided.

She looked in the telephone book and rang a number. When the sales assistant answered, she ordered some flies.

'Will you deliver them here?' she asked. 'My husband's asleep and I don't want to leave my apartment.'

'Of course,' the assistant said. 'What kind of animal are the flies for?'

'A toad.'

'Well, for a toad I suggest you also buy a small pool. And our service team will check the animal regularly, if you like. Toads sometimes develop problems with their tongues if they're fed regularly.'

'Fine,' Iran said. 'I want it to work perfectly. My husband is very fond of it.' She gave her address and hung up.

Feeling better, she made herself another cup of hot, black coffee.

GLOSSARY

admit to confess; to agree, often unwillingly, that something is true
android a robot (a complicated electronic machine) that looks like a real person
beam a line of light shining from something
brain the part of the body inside the head that controls thought, memory, and feeling
corporation a large business organization
deal a business arrangement
deer a large wild animal that eats grass, leaves, etc. and can run quickly
depression a mood of great unhappiness
emigrate to leave your country and go to live in another one
empathy the experience of feeling what another person is feeling
exist to live
fake *(adj)* not real
familiar well known; often seen or heard
form *(v)* to make into a particular shape
goat an animal with rough hair and a small beard that gives milk
hovercar a car that flies through the air
identification proof of someone's real name
laser a machine that produces a narrow, very strong beam of light
lobster a sea animal with a long body and eight legs
mind *(n)* the ability to be aware of things, and to think and to feel
nervous afraid, anxious, not confident
old-style of a type that is not modern
opera a musical play in which most of the words are sung
ostrich a large bird that can run fast but cannot fly
owl a bird with large eyes that flies and hunts at night

physical of or about the body

planet a large body in space (e.g. the Earth) that moves around a star, such as the sun

protect to keep someone or something safe from harm, injury, etc.

radioactive sending out powerful and dangerous beams that are produced when atoms are broken up

react to to change or behave in a particular way as a result of something happening

rehearse to practise songs, a play, etc. before doing it in public

religion one of the ways of believing in a supernatural power (e.g. a god or gods)

screen the part of a television, computer, etc. on which pictures and words appear

space the universe beyond the air surrounding the Earth, in which all other planets and stars exist

spider an insect with eight legs that catches flies

squirrel a small grey or brown animal that lives in trees and eats nuts

system an organized way of doing something

toad a small animal, like a frog, that lives in water and on land

truck a lorry

unite to join and act together

vote *(v)* to show your choice between different people or courses of action

wave *(n)* the movement or process by which light, heat, sound, etc. are carried

wire a long, thin piece of metal

Do Androids Dream
of Electric Sheep?

ACTIVITIES

Before Reading

1 This story has a rather mysterious title. What do you think it tells you about the story? Think of possible answers to these questions.

    1 What is an android?
    2 How can you tell the difference between an android and a human?
    3 Can androids dream? Why, or why not?
    4 Why are there electric sheep in this story?
    5 Does the story take place on Earth, or on another planet?

    Read the story introduction on the first page, and the back cover. How would you change your answers to the above questions now?

2 Read the story introduction and the back cover again. What do you think is going to happen in the story? Circle Y (Yes) or N (No) for each of these possibilities.

    1 Rick Deckard will have difficulty telling the difference between the androids and other humans. Y/N
    2 He will succeed in killing all six androids. Y/N
    3 He will earn enough money to buy himself a real living animal, instead of his electric sheep. Y/N
    4 He will feel like a murderer, become sympathetic towards the androids, and let them escape. Y/N
    5 He will give up his job and move to Mars, taking one of the androids as his servant. Y/N
    6 The androids will think faster than him, kill him, and take over San Francisco. Y/N

While Reading

Read Chapters 1 and 2. Who is speaking, and to whom? Who or what are they talking about?

1 'You're a murderer working for the police.'
2 'It's not a crime now, but I still feel like a criminal.'
3 'Male, excellent condition. Thirty thousand dollars.'
4 'Dave thinks it's accurate. Maybe it is.'
5 'We're hoping you can tell.'
6 'It's all yours. Have you decided then?'
7 'Does she know?'

Before you read Chapter 3, what do you think will happen next?

1 Will the Voigt-Kampff test help Rick to trap the androids?
2 Will Rachael Rosen work with or against Rick in future?

Read Chapters 3 and 4, and answer these questions.

1 Why were there so few people left in San Francisco?
2 Why couldn't John Isidore emigrate to Mars?
3 How did he feel when he used his empathy box?
4 What did he take as a present for his new neighbour, and what was strange about her?
5 Why did Rick refuse Rachael's offer of help?
6 Why did Max Polokov pretend to be a Russian policeman?
7 What appeared to be wrong with Rick's marriage?
8 How did Luba Luft trap Rick?

Before you read Chapter 5, can you guess the answers to these questions?

1 Which police station is real, the one on Mission Street or the one on Lombard Street? Or are they both real?
2 Is Rick really an android, with a programmed false memory? Or are Luba Luft and the police officer androids?

Read Chapters 5 and 6. Choose the best question-word for these questions, and then answer them.

How / What / Who

1 . . . did Rick persuade Garland not to shoot him?
2 . . . usually happened when an android with a false memory learned the truth about himself?
3 . . . killed Garland, and why?
4 . . . did Resch try to prove that he was not an android?
5 . . . did Luba Luft know Rick was not an android?
6 . . . were the two female androids Rick felt empathy for?
7 . . . were the names of the eight androids who came to Earth in a group from Mars?
8 . . . did Isidore feel about Pris, Roy and Irmgard, when he realized they were androids?

Before you read Chapters 7 and 8, try to guess what happens next. Choose some of these ideas.

1 Rick asks Rachael Rosen for help, and she agrees to help him.
2 Rick tries to kill Rachael, but finds he is unable to.
3 Rick can't find the last three androids, and gives up.
4 Isidore realizes the androids are using him, but doesn't care.
5 Isidore tells the police where the androids are hiding.

Read Chapters 7 and 8. Are these sentences true (T) or false (F)? Rewrite the false sentences with the correct information.

1 Rick bought the goat to give to his wife.
2 Iran believed in Mercerism more strongly than Rick did.
3 If Rick killed all the Nexus-6 androids, the Rosen Corporation would go out of business.
4 Rachael slept with Rick because she loved him.
5 Buster Friendly proved that Wilbur Mercer was a being from another planet.
6 Isidore was horrified by the androids' cruelty to the spider.

Before you read to the end, can you guess the answers to these questions?

1 Will Isidore help the androids escape, or help Rick kill them?
2 Will Rick find the androids and kill them, or will they kill him?
3 Is Wilbur Mercer real, or does he just exist in people's minds?
4 What will happen to Rick and Iran?

Read Chapters 9 and 10, and answer these questions.

1 Who warned Rick to watch out for Pris Stratton?
2 Why did the Batys let Rick into the apartment?
3 Why didn't Isidore want to live near Rick?
4 How did Rick feel about his day's work?
5 Who killed Rick's goat, and why?
6 Why did Rick fly to the Oregon desert, and what happened to him there?
7 What did Rick think his 'wrong decision' had been?
8 How did Iran feel about Rick in the end?

After Reading

1 Match the names of these characters to the pieces of information in the list below. Then select the androids, and write a short description of each one, adding any other information that you think is important.

Buster Friendly	*Phil Resch*	*Pris Stratton*	*John Isidore*
Hannibal Sloat	*Roy Baty*	*Iran Deckard*	*Max Polokov*
Rachael Rosen	*Luba Luft*	*Bill Barbour*	

human / an android / a truck driver / Rick's wife / a 'special'/ an opera singer / owned a squirrel / leader of the androids / Rick's neighbour / looked like Rachael Rosen / owner of a pet hospital / a rubbish collector / beautiful voice / voted to kill Isidore / stayed at home all day / worked for the Rosen Corporation / couldn't emigrate / owned a horse / a Russian policeman / slept with Rick Deckard / killed by Rick Deckard / cut off the spider's legs / the last to be killed / worked for the Mission Street police / a television presenter / Isidore's boss / shot by Phil Resch / killed Rick's goat / made fun of empathy boxes / often depressed

2 In the story the author describes things that we are not familiar with, but which exist in his vision of the future. What are these things, and what part did they play in the story?

- A mood machine
- An empathy box
- Sydney's catalogue
- The Voigt-Kampff test

Do you think any of these items might be in regular use in the year 2020? If so, which ones? Explain why you think this.

3 **It was probably Rachael who told Roy Baty about the deaths of the other androids (see page 59). Here is their videophone conversation. Complete Rachael's side of the conversation.**

RACHAEL: Roy, you've got to take care. There are only three of you left now.

ROY: I'd heard that Anders and Gitchel were dead. But I thought Polokov had shot the killer – what was his name?

RACHAEL: _____

ROY: So who is this other killer? Do you know him?

RACHAEL: _____

ROY: Why did he give you the V-K test? You haven't escaped from Mars. You belong to the Corporation.

RACHAEL: _____

ROY: I see. And what happened to Polokov?

RACHAEL: _____

ROY: Why didn't Luba phone Garland for help?

RACHAEL: _____

ROY: So Garland and Luba are both dead. In that case, I think Irmgard and I had better move.

RACHAEL: _____

ROY: We'll go and join Pris.

RACHAEL: _____

ROY: Yes, she sent us a card. She's in some empty apartment building in the suburbs. Listen, is this Deckard likely to get in touch with you again?

RACHAEL: _____

ROY: Well, if he does call you and ask for help, you know what to do. Give him something else to think about!

RACHAEL: _____

4 Deckard probably wrote a final report on the six killings to give to Inspector Bryant. Here is his report. Put the sentences in the right order and join them together, using the linking words, to make a paragraph of seven sentences. Start with number 5.

after / and / before / but before / but while / so / that / when / where / which / who

1 _____ they were hiding.

2 At the mysterious police station on Mission Street, I was interviewed by Garland, the third android on the list,

3 _____ I could stop him.

4 Later that evening I heard from Bryant

5 _____ searching Polokov's apartment,

6 _____ I shot him.

7 _____ was shot at his desk by Phil Resch, an android killer.

8 _____ he showed me his gun,

9 After that Resch and I went to find Luba Luft again,

10 _____ the last three androids were in an empty apartment building in the suburbs.

11 _____ annoyed Resch and he shot her

12 Then I visited the singer, Luba Luft,

13 I managed to kill one of them, Pris Stratton, on the stairs

14 _____ I could finish giving her the Voigt-Kampff test,

15 I met the Russian, Sandor Kadalyi, on the roof of the building.

16 _____ we were taking her down in the lift, she said something

17 she called the police and I was arrested.

18 _____ shot the last two, Irmgard and Roy Baty, in the apartment

19 I realized that he was in fact Max Polokov,

5 Here is a 22nd-century historian's view of Earth as described in the story. Choose one suitable word to fill each gap.

Early in the twenty-first _____, Earth lay under a _____ cloud of deadly, radioactive _____, which blocked out the _____. The world government had _____ most healthy people to _____ to Mars, but 'specials', _____ who had failed the _____ tests, were not allowed _____ emigrate or to have _____. Mercerism was the official _____, which provided, through empathy _____, experiences that people could _____ and so feel less _____. Followers of Mercerism were _____ to own and care _____ an animal, but as _____ animals were rare and _____ expensive, people often bought _____, electric ones instead and _____ that they were real.

If Earth ever did become like this, would *you* choose to emigrate to Mars? Why, or why not?

6 **The Voigt-Kampff test was designed to tell a human from an android. Look at the questions used by Rick when testing Rachael Rosen and Luba Luft (see pages 15–17, 39–40). Imagine there are dangerous Nexus-6 androids in today's world, and it is your job to trap them. What questions would *your* empathy test consist of?**

7 **What did you think of the ending? Discuss these questions.**

   1 Is there any sign of hope at the end? If so, what is it?
   2 What do you remember most at the end – the fake toad or Iran's changed behaviour towards Rick? What does that suggest?
   3 The film, *Blade Runner*, ends with Rick (who is divorced) and Rachael Rosen deciding to spend whatever is left of their lives together. Do you prefer that ending, or the one in the book? Explain why.

115

ABOUT THE AUTHOR

Philip Kindred Dick was born in Chicago in 1928, but lived most of his life in California. From 1952 to his death in 1982, he published thirty-six novels and five collections of short stories, and his science-fiction writing is still hugely popular. He had a painful emotional life, starting with the death of his twin sister forty-one days after birth, and continuing through several bad marriages, to a long period of drug addiction. A turning-point came in Canada in 1972. He tried to kill himself, but stopped in time, and then began working with teenagers to help them give up drugs. This eventually brought him out of his depression.

Much of his personal experience appears in his writing. As he said, 'I am, by profession, a science fiction writer. I deal in fantasy. My life is a fantasy.' He was constantly exploring how far human ideas of life, death, religion, and love could survive in a dark, uncaring world, and spoke of 'the need for people who were human to reinforce other people's humanness . . . to rebel against an inhuman or android society.'

His best-known titles include *The Man in the High Castle* (1962), *Martian Time-Slip* (1964), *A Scanner Darkly* (1977), and of course, *Do Androids Dream of Electric Sheep?* (1968). The famous 1982 film *Blade Runner* was based on this novel. Set in Los Angeles instead of San Francisco, the film concentrates on the hunting and killing of the androids by the tough policeman known as Blade Runner (played by Harrison Ford). It is a powerful film, now regarded as a classic, but the novel is more complex, taking the reader through the dark places of the human mind and turning reality inside out.

OXFORD BOOKWORMS LIBRARY

Classics • Crime & Mystery • Factfiles • Fantasy & Horror
Human Interest • Playscripts • Thriller & Adventure
True Stories • World Stories

The OXFORD BOOKWORMS LIBRARY provides enjoyable reading in English, with a wide range of classic and modern fiction, non-fiction, and plays. It includes original and adapted texts in seven carefully graded language stages, which take learners from beginner to advanced level. An overview is given on the next pages.

All Stage 1 titles are available as audio recordings, as well as over eighty other titles from Starter to Stage 6. All Starters and many titles at Stages 1 to 4 are specially recommended for younger learners. Every Bookworm is illustrated, and Starters and Factfiles have full-colour illustrations.

The OXFORD BOOKWORMS LIBRARY also offers extensive support. Each book contains an introduction to the story, notes about the author, a glossary, and activities. Additional resources include tests and worksheets, and answers for these and for the activities in the books. There is advice on running a class library, using audio recordings, and the many ways of using Oxford Bookworms in reading programmes. Resource materials are available on the website <www.oup.com/elt/bookworms>.

The *Oxford Bookworms Collection* is a series for advanced learners. It consists of volumes of short stories by well-known authors, both classic and modern. Texts are not abridged or adapted in any way, but carefully selected to be accessible to the advanced student.

You can find details and a full list of titles in the *Oxford Bookworms Library Catalogue* and *Oxford English Language Teaching Catalogues*, and on the website <www.oup.com/elt/bookworms>.

THE OXFORD BOOKWORMS LIBRARY
GRADING AND SAMPLE EXTRACTS

STARTER • 250 HEADWORDS

present simple – present continuous – imperative –
can/cannot, must – *going to* (future) – simple gerunds …

Her phone is ringing – but where is it?

Sally gets out of bed and looks in her bag. No phone. She looks under the bed. No phone. Then she looks behind the door. There is her phone. Sally picks up her phone and answers it. *Sally's Phone*

STAGE 1 • 400 HEADWORDS

… past simple – coordination with *and, but, or* –
subordination with *before, after, when, because, so* …

I knew him in Persia. He was a famous builder and I worked with him there. For a time I was his friend, but not for long. When he came to Paris, I came after him – I wanted to watch him. He was a very clever, very dangerous man. *The Phantom of the Opera*

STAGE 2 • 700 HEADWORDS

… present perfect – *will* (future) – *(don't) have to, must not, could* –
comparison of adjectives – simple *if* clauses – past continuous –
tag questions – *ask/tell* + infinitive …

While I was writing these words in my diary, I decided what to do. I must try to escape. I shall try to get down the wall outside. The window is high above the ground, but I have to try. I shall take some of the gold with me – if I escape, perhaps it will be helpful later. *Dracula*

STAGE 3 • 1000 HEADWORDS

... should, may – present perfect continuous – *used to* – past perfect –
causative – relative clauses – indirect statements ...

Of course, it was most important that no one should see
Colin, Mary, or Dickon entering the secret garden. So Colin
gave orders to the gardeners that they must all keep away
from that part of the garden in future. *The Secret Garden*

STAGE 4 • 1400 HEADWORDS

... past perfect continuous – passive (simple forms) –
would conditional clauses – indirect questions –
relatives with *where/when* – gerunds after prepositions/phrases ...

I was glad. Now Hyde could not show his face to the world
again. If he did, every honest man in London would be proud
to report him to the police. *Dr Jekyll and Mr Hyde*

STAGE 5 • 1800 HEADWORDS

... future continuous – future perfect –
passive (modals, continuous forms) –
would have conditional clauses – modals + perfect infinitive ...

If he had spoken Estella's name, I would have hit him. I was so
angry with him, and so depressed about my future, that I could
not eat the breakfast. Instead I went straight to the old house.
Great Expectations

STAGE 6 • 2500 HEADWORDS

... passive (infinitives, gerunds) – advanced modal meanings –
clauses of concession, condition

When I stepped up to the piano, I was confident. It was as if I
knew that the prodigy side of me really did exist. And when I
started to play, I was so caught up in how lovely I looked that
I didn't worry how I would sound. *The Joy Luck Club*

I, Robot – Short Stories

ISAAC ASIMOV

Retold by Rowena Akinyemi

A human being is a soft, weak creature. It needs constant supplies of air, water, and food; it has to spend a third of its life asleep, and it can't work if the temperature is too hot or too cold.

But a robot is made of strong metal. It uses electrical energy directly, never sleeps, and can work in any temperature. It is stronger, more efficient – and sometimes more human than human beings.

Isaac Asimov was one of the greatest science-fiction writers, and these short stories give us an unforgettable and terrifying vision of the future.

The Accidental Tourist

ANNE TYLER

Retold by Jennifer Bassett

Everyday life in Baltimore, USA, is full of problems – getting the washing done, buying groceries and dog food, avoiding the neighbors . . . After the death of his son and the departure of his wife, Macon's attempts to run his own life become increasingly desperate – and more and more odd.

Meanwhile, he has to get on with his work, writing tourist guides for business people. Then his dog Edward starts to bite people, and he has to send for Muriel, the dog trainer. And day by day, Macon's life gets more and more complicated.